Free Markets Under Siege

Cartels, Politics and Social Welfare

D1482343

Free Markets Under Siege

Free Markets Under Siege

Cartels, Politics and Social Welfare

RICHARD A. EPSTEIN

THIRTY-THIRD WINCOTT LECTURE

13 OCTOBER 2003

WITH A COMMENTARY BY GEOFFREY E. WOOD

The Institute of Economic Affairs

First published in Great Britain in 2004 by
The Institute of Economic Affairs
2 Lord North Street
Westminster
London SW1P 3LB
in association with Profile Books Ltd

The mission of the Institute of Economic Affairs is to improve public
understanding of the fundamental institutions of a free society, with particular
reference to the role of markets in solving economic and social problems.

Copyright © The Wincott Foundation 2004

The moral right of the authors has been asserted.

All rights reserved. Without limiting the rights under copyright reserved above,
no part of this publication may be reproduced, stored or introduced into a
retrieval system, or transmitted, in any form or by any means (electronic,
mechanical, photocopying, recording or otherwise), without the prior written
permission of both the copyright owner and the publisher of this book.

A CIP catalogue record for this book is available from the British Library.

ISBN 0 255 36553 5

Many IEA publications are translated into languages other than English or
are reprinted. Permission to translate or to reprint should be sought from the
Director General at the address above.

Typeset in Stone by MacGuru Ltd
info@macguru.org.uk

Printed and bound in Great Britain by Hobbs the Printers

CONTENTS

THE AUTHOR

Richard A. Epstein is the James Parker Hall Distinguished Service Professor of Law at the University of Chicago, where he has taught since 1972. He has also been the Peter and Kirstin Senior Fellow at the Hoover Institution since 2000. Prior to joining the University of Chicago Law School faculty, he taught law at the University of Southern California from 1968 to 1972. He served as Interim Dean of the University of Chicago Law School from February to June 2001. In 2003 he received an LL D, *honoris causa*, from the University of Ghent. He has been a member of the American Academy of Arts and Sciences since 1985 and a Senior Fellow of the Center for Clinical Medical Ethics at the University of Chicago Medical School since 1983. From 1981 to 1991 he served as editor of the *Journal of Legal Studies*, and from 1991 to 2001 as editor of the *Journal of Law and Economics*. At present he is a director of the John M. Olin Program in Law and Economics. His books include *Skepticism and Freedom: A Modern Case for Classical Liberalism* (University of Chicago, 2003); *Cases and Materials on Torts* (Aspen Law & Business, 8th edn, 2004); *Torts* (Aspen Law & Business, 1999); *Principles for a Free Society: Reconciling Individual Liberty with the Common Good* (Perseus Books, 1998); *Mortal Peril: Our Inalienable Rights to Health Care?* (Addison-Wesley, 1997); *Simple Rules for a Complex World* (Harvard, 1995); *Bargaining with the State* (Princeton, 1993); *Forbidden Grounds: The Case against*

Employment Discrimination Laws (Harvard, 1992); *Takings: Private Property and the Power of Eminent Domain* (Harvard, 1985); and *Modern Products Liability Law* (Greenwood Press, 1980).

He has written numerous articles on a wide range of legal and interdisciplinary subjects, and has taught courses in civil procedure, communications, conflicts of laws, constitutional law, contracts, corporations, criminal law, jurisprudence, health law and policy, legal history, property, real estate development and finance, labour law, land use planning, patents, individual, estate and corporate taxation, Roman Law, torts, and workers' compensation.

FOREWORD

One of the aims of the Wincott Foundation is to contribute to a better understanding of how markets work, and to highlight the damage that can be caused to social welfare when market forces are suppressed to serve the narrow aims of special interest groups. These themes figured prominently in the writings of Harold Wincott, the financial journalist in whose honour the Foundation was set up in 1960, and they have been articulated in several of the Wincott Lectures which have been held annually since that date.

The 2003 Wincott Lecture, delivered by Professor Richard Epstein from the University of Chicago and published in extended form in this paper, provides an illuminating analysis of some of the ways in which interest groups, aided and abetted by sympathetic politicians, have been able to rig the market in their favour. The lecturer focuses in particular on two areas where such intervention has been extensive and persistent in the USA and western Europe – agriculture and the labour market.

On the first, Professor Epstein shows how the 'right to farm', proclaimed by President Franklin Roosevelt in his 1944 State of the Union address, was transformed into the right of an individual to remain indefinitely in a particular occupation, whatever changes in supply and demand might take place; these arrangements were bolstered by an elaborate array of subsidies and restrictions designed to preserve the status quo – at considerable cost to taxpayers and consumers. While the damage has been offset, at least in the advanced industrial countries, by spectacular improvements in agricultural productivity, Professor Epstein points out that the gains from technology are not spread evenly around the world and that agricultural protection imposes great damage on developing countries, which are prevented from making full use of their advantages of climate and cheap labour.

As for the labour market, the lecture contains a fascinating account of how pro-competitive rulings by the US Supreme Court in 1908 and 1917 were subsequently undermined by political decisions to exempt trade unions from the scope of the anti-trust laws and then to regulate collective bargaining through the National Labour Relations Act; the consequence was the statutory codification of monopoly over competition. Fortunately, the effect of these measures was somewhat blunted by the Taft-Hartley Act of 1947, which restricted the ability of unions to bring pressure on employers through secondary boycotts and in other ways. Even more important was the impact of foreign competition: the postwar change in public attitudes towards free trade has had a strong market-positive influence on the degree of trade union power.

Professor Epstein relates these cases to the larger issue of how best to regulate the interface between market choice and government behaviour. Drawing on his deep knowledge of history, law and economics, he discusses the need to find a middle way between socialism and libertarianism. The libertarians, he suggests, have got many things right, not least in their stress on the social gains that arise from voluntary exchange, but they sometimes underplay the importance of the social infrastructure – including a system of public taxation and finance – that no market can supply.

The great challenge for liberal democracies is to work out how to use systems of coercion to benefit the individuals and institutions subjected to it. In the lecturer's view, it is possible to devise rules that permit the provision of public goods without allowing the state to succumb to the political favouritism that leads to massive transfers of wealth from one faction to another.

Professor Epstein presents his arguments with clarity, force and wit – qualities that were very much in evidence during the lively discussion that followed his lecture. The trustees of the Wincott Foundation are grateful to Professor Epstein for agreeing to deliver the lecture, and warmly commend this paper.

As with all IEA publications, the views expressed in Professor Epstein's paper are those of the author, not those of the Institute (which has no corporate view), its managing trustees, Academic Advisory Council members or senior staff.

SIR GEOFFREY OWEN

Chairman of the Trustees,
The Wincott Foundation
February 2004

ACKNOWLEDGEMENTS

A lecture and a manuscript may have but a single author, but they are always works of collaboration. I should therefore like to thank Geoffrey Owen for asking me to give this lecture, and working with me on the selection of a topic; Geoffrey Wood for writing his commentary on my remarks; and Eric Murphy, University of Chicago Law School, class of 2005, for his exceptional help in working through the problems in preparing this manuscript.

RICHARD EPSTEIN
Stanford, California

The front cover

The front cover shows an illustration by David Bromley that accompanied my op-ed piece, entitled 'Free Markets Demand Protection', in the *Financial Times* of 13 October 2003. It is reproduced here by permission of the *Financial Times*. The drawing's complex imagery was intended to illustrate a point which was a central theme of the article and this Wincott Lecture – namely, that it is important to pick the low-hanging fruit first, before attempting more complex manoeuvres to gather the fruit hanging higher up. In concrete terms this means deal with social order first, and then – within the economic realm – protect open markets from the multitude of protectionist impulses that lie in wait to subvert them.

EXECUTIVE SUMMARY

- There are particular decisions that politicians have the power to make which have a profound impact on economic well-being. These are 'easy cases' and include issues such as free trade and the freedom to contract.
- There are other policy decisions that are 'hard cases' where it is difficult to devise the optimal policy and the impact of a sub-optimal policy will be relatively minor compared with getting the 'easy cases' wrong.
- Economists and politicians should concentrate on getting the 'easy cases' right but there are, in practice, many areas where governments continue to get 'easy cases' wrong. Obvious examples are in labour market regulation and intervention in agricultural markets – existing policy has huge costs to society.
- A fundamental principle of economic policy in a free society is that there should be no compensation for 'competitive harm' – that is, for harm caused not by the violation of property but by economic competition.
- Paradoxically, the conditions needed for perfect competition to exist are the same as the conditions required for the effective cartelisation of markets. The most important of these is the standardisation of products.
- Agricultural protection began in the 1930s in the USA as a

result of the post-New Deal 'right to farm' legislation. This did not mean 'freedom to farm' in the normal sense of the word but imposed a duty on others to ensure that a farmer could make a given income from the chosen occupation regardless of economic conditions. Different legislative structures with similar effects were developed in the EU. In effect farmers are compensated for losses resulting from competition.

- Reform of agricultural protection, returning it to the normal processes of competition, would bring big economic gains – even if such reform were unilateral.
- The normal principles of law relating both to freedom of contract and to protecting consumers against cartels have been completely inverted in the case of labour markets. Again the same trends are evident in both the USA and the EU.
- Economists need to win the major intellectual battle on the importance of competition and apply that reasoning to markets such as those for labour and agriculture. If they do not, forces may develop that will engulf capitalist economies.

Free Markets Under Siege

Cartels, Politics and Social Welfare

1 MODERN JUSTIFICATION FOR CLASSICAL LIBERALISM

It was a very great honour to be invited to give the Wincott Lecture for 2003, for it allows me to renew a set of connections that I have long had with England. I started my legal education in Oxford in 1964, receiving a BA in Jurisprudence in 1966, after which I returned to the USA to complete my legal education at Yale in 1968. Immediately upon graduation, I took up the study and teaching of law, which became my life's work. The combination of English and American education has proved a great advantage to me because it familiarised me with *three* legal systems: English and American are the obvious two; the Roman law system, which was then required study at Oxford, is the third. The English educational experience was essential to my intellectual development, but not perhaps as my instructors intended, for they nourished my affection for the laissez-faire tradition more by happenstance than conscious design. The major questions in English law, then as now, are often resolved by administrative order within the vaunted Civil Service, which translated into the (then) regnant rule of English administrative law that all decisions of the minister should be final. The effect, therefore, was that in our curriculum we concentrated on those matters that did not fall into the purview of the minister's discretion in the administrative state. In effect, the legal education placed its emphasis on private law as it governed the unregulated portion of the economy. That project in turn required us to read a large number of 19th-century and earlier decisions written by judges who were congenial to voluntary contract and private property. At the same time, my study of Roman law persuaded me that the basic principles of English common law could also take hold in political settings widely different from those in modern times.

Unlike political theorists who work at an abstract level, these judges had the huge advantage of testing their basic theories against the concrete cases that cried out for decision. By the same token, these same judges often suffered from a professional disadvantage because, with a few notable exceptions, they did not ground their views in general political theory. Indeed, it is on that score that English legal education has lagged somewhat, both then and now, for it does not place enough emphasis on the importance of inter-disciplinary studies, which have been the centrepiece of American legal education for several decades at least. But an English and an American legal education proved, in my case, to be happily complementary.

Having learned from two cultures, I regard my comparative advantage in this intellectual debate as the ability to work as an intellectual arbitrageur between the two worlds, for in time I came to believe that the rules of decision in these private disputes had real relevance to the larger questions that had in practice been taken over by the modern administrative state. The conclusions, moreover, seemed to hold with equal force in the USA, notwithstanding the two very great differences between our legal systems: the US written constitution and federalism are linked features, as yet nowhere found in England. I hope that, armed with the tools of economics and political theory, I can produce theoretical arguments that better explain the social desirability of certain institutions than the ancient appeal to 'natural reason'. That term, which had its origin in the Roman texts, worked well enough in ages past when intuition was the dominant guide to the formation of legal policy. It counted as the dominant intellectual motif for such great political and legal writers as Grotius, Locke, Pufendorf and Blackstone, who have exerted such an enormous positive influence in modern times. But now that we have developed a stronger apparatus of economic and political theory, that form of theoretical quiescence can no longer carry the day. There is so much to say about social institutions and laws that it becomes foolhardy to regard self-evidence as the ultimate criterion of a sound legal rule, political institution or social practice. We have to use the most modern logic and theory available, whether we want to or not, for our adversaries, whoever they may be, will rightly do the same on the other side. Fortunately, the use of the new techniques usually proves benevolent in that it helps us to justify in a modern idiom the results of these earlier writers in terms more robust than they could supply for their own deeply held intuitions. Our job, therefore, is neither to junk their conclusions nor to belittle their efforts. It is to engage in an intelligent reconstruction of great ideas that have withstood the test of time.

My more immediate connection with England relates directly to Harold Wincott and the *Financial Times*. It leads to one of the central themes of this lecture. The *FT* was kind enough to publish an article of mine in its issue of 13 October 2003. It begins with a picture that relates to the topic of this talk – first gather the low-hanging fruit – but which, I fear, not even the most astute reader could decipher. The picture shows a tree with a lot of apples. On one side, there are people standing on the ground, reaching out and grabbing the apples; on the other stand people with ladders and hoists trying to figure out how they can climb up to gather the apples at the top of the tree. The obvious query is: what on earth does a picture of a tree with a collection of apples have to do with the question of how to organise different markets? As I looked at the illustration, I would have said that the picture contained an oblique reference to the temptation and fall of Adam and Eve as evidence that the private appropriation of natural resources is the source of all evil in the world. But my column had no such devious intention. To clarify matters, therefore, I will take a moment to explain what the picture is about because in fact it highlights the central theme of this lecture: first and foremost, get the easy cases right, and then worry about the hard cases later.

Here is how I reached this conclusion. The study of any complex social system leads on reflection to the comforting observation that the world contains easy as well as hard cases. The following characteristics are true of hard cases: they require a huge expenditure of intellectual energy in order to figure out their solution, yet, measured against some social ideal, our best choices invariably suffer from a very high rate of error even when we do our level best. The happy side of this process is that we are likely to be damned no matter which alternative we embrace. So if the law seeks to determine a very complicated issue such as the optimum duration of a patent, it is easy to identify an infinite set of permutations. The question of patent duration cannot be effect-ively decided in isolation, without reference to patent scope, itself a highly technical area. To make matters worse, the field of patent-able inventions might be too broad for a general solution to the problem. The answer that seems to work well for pharmaceutical patents may not be as sensible for software. But the moment we decide that different patents classes should have different lengths, someone will be faced with the unhappy task of classifying a new generation of inventions that regrettably straddles a pre-existing set of categories established in ignorance of the future path of technical development: such is the case with computer software, for example. Given this shifting background, it is very difficult to authoritatively conclude that one patent length rather than another is the best. Of course, we can make credible arguments that patent duration should be far shorter than copyright duration, but that does not fix an appropriate length for either form of intellectual property. In the end, the best answers rely on educated hunches by persons who work within the field, who may differ substantially in their conclusions.

In some cases the problems get even more difficult than patent duration because of the discontinuous nature of the basic choice. All too often, the world does not allow us the luxury of continually fine-tuning responses until we approach some social ideal. The question of whether to build a new airport or highway or rail system gives rise to an initial 'yes or no' choice. Once that basic commitment is made, it will of course be followed by a host of smaller decisions, some of which can be fine-tuned but others not. The advantages and disadvantages of the basic choice are hard to foresee and are equally hard to evaluate quantitatively even when foreseen. Just think of how hard it is to estimate the impact of a new airport on noise, pollution, traffic, land values, business growth and the like. The only thing we can say with certainty is that some affected persons will win and others will lose. Yet it is no mean feat to examine which persons fall into which class, or to determine how much compensation, if any, is owing to those persons who are inconvenienced by the process. The difficulty of the subject matter and the nature of the political process restrict us to sharply discontinuous solutions, all of which could be far removed from the social ideal. Any choice is likely to contain large errors. But the same is not necessarily true of the *difference* in errors between two solutions. That figure could be small. Thus, if one error goes high by 1,000 and the other low by 1,000, the error levels could be enormous, but equally balanced. In the midst of our travail, we ought to take comfort in the thought that so long as people do their level best to get the hard cases right, then we should not protest too loudly if they get them wrong. The chances are that other people would have made similar mistakes, and we will never get able people to work on difficult social projects as long as we insist on judging their handiwork harshly with the benefit of hindsight. Our standard of criticism has to respect the decisions made in good faith by persons in positions of responsibility, so that they are not hauled into the dock when it appears that they made the wrong decision, a principle which lies at the core of the doctrine of official immunity. We have to learn to both live and prosper in a second-best world.

The appropriate response to hard cases, then, is an uneasy mix between patience and deference. The easy cases, in contrast, turn out to be miraculously important for the day-to-day operations of any system precisely because we can be confident that the wrong decision will lead to serious social dislocations with few offsetting benefits. This proposition holds for how a society draws the interface between market choice and government behaviour, which is my main theme. But once again we have to keep the basic point about economic organisation in perspective. The truly great social catastrophes do not arise from a misapplication of the basic principles of a market economy. They arise from a wholesale disrespect for individual liberty, which is manifested in tolerated lynchings and arbitrary arrest, and from a total contempt for private property, through its outright seizure by government forces intent on stifling its opposition or lining its own pockets. The reason why Great Britain and the USA did not go the way of Germany and the Soviet Union in the turmoil of the 1930s was that the political institutions in both our countries were able to hold firm against these palpable excesses even as they went astray on a host of smaller economic issues.

It was the failure to grasp this point clearly that led Hayek (1944) to be too gloomy about the fate of democratic institutions in western Europe and the USA. Socialism does not always lead to national socialism, as these critical minimum conditions for political freedom are respected across the political spectrum. Once this distinction is kept in mind, it becomes clear why we can properly count Franklin D. Roosevelt as a great American president on the political frontier even while taking strong exception, as I shall do in this lecture, to the misguided economic polices that permeated his New Deal. His contemporary competition in the category of world historical figures was Adolf Hitler, Josef Stalin, Mao Zedong and Chiang Kai-shek. In that group, Roosevelt, along with Churchill, stands tall as a beacon of liberty in a world that had plunged into disaster. Conrad Black (2003) may well be right to hail Roosevelt as a great figure, and even as the saviour of capitalism. But his success on the political level should not blind us to his shortfalls on the matters of economic and legal policy, especially on the matters of agriculture and labour, which are the central theme of this lecture.

2 BETWEEN SOCIALISM AND LIBERTARIANISM

On the question of what is the proper form for organising the means of production, to use the Marxist phrase, there is a wide range of disagreement over whether a system of voluntary, competitive, markets will supply the best mix of goods and services to the population at large. Even if we remember not to elevate this issue to a matter of life and death, by the same token we should not veer too far in the opposite direction by lapsing into a form of economic fatalism, which holds that society's social ills will remain at some constant level no matter what kind of economic system we adopt. On the contrary, the level of social prosperity, and with it political peace, depend heavily on the answers that we collectively give to these economic and legal issues. Getting the issues right in the easy cases should not be greeted with stony indifference, even in comparison with the larger political issues we face.

'Easy cases' and 'difficult cases'

In delineating the proper role for the market and the state, it is vital for people who believe, as I do and as Harold Wincott did, in the principles of liberal democracy to get the easy cases right even if they cannot reach firm agreement on the difficult questions such as patent scope and airport location. In this spirit, I shall now concentrate on these easy cases and put the harder cases to one side. I hope to show how, far from reaching the appropriate classical liberal solutions to these problems, our political institutions frequently (but thankfully not universally) do everything backwards, often in the worst possible manner. Institutional arrangements that should be a dull subject, not worthy of any discourse or conversation, become the object of intensive study in economic pathology to explain how societies first make one wrong step only to follow that mistake with others, setting in motion a downward cycle that creates unnecessary social losses all along the way.

In order to frame this part of the argument, I think it is important to articulate the proper baseline for analysis. In my new book, *Skepticism and Freedom* (Epstein 2003), I defend, as I have done for many years, a vision of classical liberalism that avoids two kinds of perils. One is the peril associated with an unyielding devotion to an unvarnished and incautious libertarian philosophy. On the other side lies the greater peril that comes from embracing socialism or collectivism in all its forms. The issue is how to find the middle way between these two extremes.

I should not need to dwell at length on the weaknesses of collectivism as a system for controlling the means of production. It should suffice to note that no individual has either the knowledge or the selflessness to make vital decisions for other individuals. The high aspirations of collective ownership are always dashed by the grubby particulars of its practical realisation. But this simple point has not always carried the day, so a few more words are needed on the topic. In particular, it is instructive to recall the powerful claims that were voiced on its behalf during the socialist calculation debate of the 1930s and 1940s. The basic claim was that a large computer could generate all the information about what goods and services should be produced under what conditions. Markets were not thought of as generative institutions, so the hope was that state planners could rig the rules of the game to approximate the ideal mix of goods and services that markets (are supposed to) generate, which could then be happily married to an income policy that narrowed the gap between rich and poor.

It is a tribute to the work of Friedrich Hayek that today no one quite believes that this fantasy could be brought to successful completion, even though computers are a billion times more efficient today than they were when the socialist calculation debate took place. This utopian proposal is doomed to failure because all interested parties in the planning debacle, both public and private, will have equal access to these devices, no matter how powerful. As the night follows the day, every clever government intervention will invite multiple private responses, which are certain to undo whatever good might have come about if dedicated government officials (itself a generous assumption) had exclusive use of the new technologies involved. The hope that we could keep the distribution, be it of income or wealth, on one axis and the production of goods and services on a second axis, such that the twain will never meet, has disappeared into the dustbin of history. The single strongest safeguard that we have against excessive planning stems from the awareness that any government initiative, however noble, marks only the first step in what promises to be a long and arduous multiple period game – a game in which it is hard to say with confidence that any one player could emerge victorious. Caution with respect to means may well slow down individuals and groups that maintain strong collective ideals about the choice of ends, most notably the compression of income differentials through social planning.

The argument today, therefore, has switched grounds. No

longer is it said that the state can outperform the market. Rather it is said that the market itself suffers from certain 'failures' that justify forms of state intervention to protect individuals who are hurt in the process. The movement towards collectivisation of all public activities, if it is to take place today, will not rest on a single bold initiative that casts aside the private sector. Rather, it will take place in the form of a multiple attack along different margins, where each individual struggle does not generalise easily across the board. The long-standing objective of the modern closet socialist is to consolidate the separate beachheads after they are taken over. Thus, state dominance can be portrayed as a device that takes the irrationality, impersonality and cruelty out of markets, and not as a device that dispenses with their use altogether. In effect, the discourse takes the form of an intellectual two-step. Step one: markets are all right when they work. Step two: but markets do not work in this particular area, be it healthcare, labour, housing, agriculture or whatever, each with its 'special' problems. In one sense, the quiet blessing in this approach is that it obviates the risk of a catastrophic conversion to state control through aggressive nationalisation. But it gives rise to a multiple-front war in which substantial chunks of voluntary markets always find themselves at risk. The case against overall socialism is irrefutable today. But the desire to keep up with its egalitarian objectives continues to exert a considerable influence in practice. There is little reason to think that the intellectual foundations of the collective impulse are strong enough to serve as the foundation for a more viable and comprehensive philosophy. But we still have to keep in mind the importance that market failures have when it comes to the analysis of the libertarian alternative.

Strengths and weaknesses of libertarian thought

Even if socialism may be dispatched in a few sentences, it is far more profitable to devote some words to the commendable strengths and serious drawbacks of libertarian thought. We will start with the positives, then move on to the limitations. Without question, the sensible libertarian understands the importance of property rights, understands the importance of voluntary exchange, and understands the importance of keeping to a minimum state devices that could upset the precarious balance created by strong property institutions. The presumption against the use of state power means that libertarians are rightly sensitive to the problems associated with the use of force on the one hand and the various kinds of deception that individuals can play upon each other on the other. The good libertarian does not fall into the socialist trap of thinking that any individual can rise above human failings only when they are placed in a position of high power, where in fact the temptations are likely to intensify. Rather, they start with a reasonably astute estimation of human character. The libertarian is not somebody who believes that we are all dewy-eyed individuals who will always work for the best interests of other people. Rather, he recognises that self-interest is a force that sometimes can be turned to bad ends and sometimes to good ends. Armed with that knowledge, he tries to figure out how to minimise the bad consequences of human action and maximise the good.

The basic commandment of this approach, with which I agree, is that voluntary transactions are presumptively preferred because they are positive-sum games from which both sides benefit. In contrast, the use of fraud and coercion are regarded with deep suspicion because these are pure transfer games in which one side may benefit (somewhat) and the other side will lose (a great deal more). We need some way to net out the pluses and the minuses of coercive transactions. On this score, the sombre conclusion is that the minuses are likely to dominate simply because people are less likely to resort to theft when they can organise a voluntary transaction that works to their mutual advantage. When they resort to force and deception they surely pay a price, but it is likely to be far lower than the harm that they inflict on others whose lives, limbs and fortunes are placed at risk. On these critical points the insights of libertarian theory cannot be ignored, even if they may have to be qualified.

The second point that the libertarian rightly grasps is that one good idea, voluntary exchange, applied multiple times, becomes a truly great idea. If law sets up a system in which two parties make a transaction, each can take what he receives in any given exchange and decide to consume it, to invest it or to resell it to a third person. The more rapid the velocity of transactions, the more likely that all individuals will exhaust the full set of gains available from the contractual process. Mutual gain is, therefore, piled on top of mutual gain in transactions that involve two, or more, persons. In seeking to understand private contracts, it is always a mistake to think of them as one-shot transactions in a stagnant economy. Rather, it is a dynamic system in which the ceaseless exchange of goods and services generates positive consequences for other people whose opportunities are enhanced by the greater wealth and prosperity of their neighbours. The point is that a system of private property and voluntary exchange does produce a fair share of externalities, but to the extent that these are routinely positive, not negative, the externalities give truth to the old proposition of the late John F. Kennedy that a rising tide raises all ships. Quite simply, so long as all individuals can participate in the operation of a market system, no tiny group of individuals will be able to corner the wealth – and, through it, the well-being – that it generates.

Unlike the model of socialism, the libertarian position has positive features that must be incorporated in any more comprehensive view of the world. This model tallies so well with our ordinary experiential base that it is easy, almost too easy, to think that it offers the full solution to our social problem. After all, there is much to be said for a system that allows complex social organisations – commercial, social and charitable – to arise out of a sequence of voluntary transactions that recombine initial endowments of property and labour in packages that work to the long-term advantage of all their participants. The point of vulnerability of this system, however, is that it cannot generate from its own premises the background social conditions that allow it to flourish. A system of property rights requires the enforcement of the boundaries that keep persons apart. Self-help is one possible solution to this problem, but that is a mantle that can be claimed by aggressors as well as by their victims. Self-declarations will not allow us to sort out these two groups one from the other. Nor will it be easy to find a market solution to this problem, for every side to a dispute (many of which involve more than two individuals) will demand some control over the choice of the final referee. It is because of this void that we have the need for (and fear of) a single institution to make authoritative decisions about the rights and duties of the various individuals and firms within a complex society. We thus find ourselves in the unhappy situation of demanding some sort of state monopoly to enforce the rights that make a decentralised economic system possible. Indeed, the ambiguities go deeper than all this, for voluntary transactions and private property take place on top of a social infrastructure that no market can supply.

On this point, I am always impressed by market-oriented writers such as Hernando de Soto (1989 and 2000) who start with the social necessity of having a single state-run system that allows market economies to flourish. His simplest example is that of ordinary street addresses, without which it is not possible to organise a system for delivering the mail or supplying electricity, gas, police and fire services.

This simple commitment to a legal and physical infrastructure requires a system of public taxation and finance. These institutions cannot operate strictly and solely on the basis of voluntary cooperation, given that virtually all (self-interested) individuals will have the tendency to let others pick up the lion's share of the cost from the collective institutions from which they hope to benefit (see, for example, Olson 1965). Public-spirited individuals are too few and far between to pick up the slack. Unfortunately, everyone cannot simply stand back from collective responsibilities in the vain hope that necessary public services will somehow be supplied by others. Hence, the great challenge in liberal democracies is to figure out how to use a system of coercion to benefit the very individuals and institutions subjected to it. Stated otherwise, the public provision of any goods and services necessarily presupposes a system of public taxation and finance. In order for these funds to be intelligently spent, we need to develop a sound collective judgement as to which infrastructure projects are worth undertaking and which are not. If the libertarian holds fast to the assumption that all forms of state coercion are equal, then he strips himself of the tools that might allow him to segregate out those state projects that are worth doing and those which are not. Likewise, the rejection of all systems of taxation makes it impossible to distinguish between better and worse systems of taxation and exposes a serious political theory to the most dangerous of refutations – ridicule.

There is a bright side, however. Once we recognise that private markets need these public systems, then we can at least develop a criterion by which we should judge the public use of force: does the use of coercion benefit those who are subject to the taxes and regulations that the government imposes? Stated in a single sentence, the key weakness of the hard libertarian position is that it does not make room for situations where property is, and ought to be, taken, be it by occupation, regulation or taxation, in exchange for just compensation, be it in cash or in the form of in-kind benefits such as the increased security of private property and voluntary transactions. This immense area of forced exchanges does not concede an 'open sesame' to state power. Rather, it is hemmed in with serious limitations on what state actions may be undertaken, and towards what end, and what forms of compensation should be supplied. I have written of these subjects at length elsewhere (see Epstein 1985 and 1993). Suffice to say it is possible to devise rules that do permit the provision of needed public goods without allowing the state to succumb to political favouritism that leads to massive transfers of wealth from one political faction to another. The candid response to the challenge of forced exchanges to the provision of public (i.e. non-divisible and non-exclusive) goods is what the standard libertarian theory most critically lacks. It is for this reason that I often prefer the label classical liberal, on the ground that the basic theory recognises the need for some government role that libertarians may acknowledge but their stripped-down theories cannot fully explain.

Competitive markets and compensation for competitive harms

Rather than pursue this thorny topic here, I am approaching this lecture in a more simple-minded mood. I want to address the easy cases that do not depend on the complex conceptions of public goods and just compensation that play so large a role in markets such as transportation and communication, so that the differences between the libertarian and the classical liberal are for this exercise at least relatively unimportant. More concretely, my objective is to return to those many markets where we do not have to worry about these massive coordination problems precisely because two individuals can enter into exchanges that promote their mutual gain even if they are unable to secure the cooperation or participation of anyone else. Where, then, does the simple logic of voluntary contracting lead us to in this connection?

Clearly, this world is not devoid of problems. In any exchange between two persons, it is important to ask whether it is truly voluntary or whether it is subject to duress, fraud or some other form of undue influence. This will certainly be an issue in transactions that involve medical treatment for old or infirm persons whose cognitive capacities are sharply limited. Indeed, much of the debate in medical ethics relates to the question of what should be done in situations where people are at best marginally competent to make critical decisions about their own future. But the concerns that permeate certain specialised transactions are, thankfully, not a serious concern in most organised markets. Undue influence is not a real issue in mercantile transactions that take place on open exchanges. These trades usually work just as the textbook says they should: they produce benefits to the two traders, which in turn set up opportunities for a third person to profit as well.

So the basic situation leaves us in the best of all possible worlds, where a local improvement between two parties is accompanied by a generalised form of social improvement. But it is here that our difficulties begin, for any successful trade may often leave in its wake one or more disappointed competitors who are worse off in this particular instance because of their inability to make the sale. Their competitive loss is a real economic harm, and it is always possible for individuals to ignore the systematic gains from trade and insist that they should receive some sort of compensation for their competitive loss.

It is on this big, easy question that the rubber hits the road, for everyone who is committed to the classical liberal position will fight to the death against the compensation for losses arising in a competitive economy, notwithstanding the fierce resistance they routinely encounter in practice. The common argument is that economic losses from competition are every bit as real to their victims as those that result from the use of force. If we allow compensation for physical injuries, and injunctions against their future occurrence, then we should do the same for competitive losses, which should likewise be enjoined or compensated.

As I noted earlier, the classical writers on this subject rejected these claims, and they did so with a Latin phrase, *damnum absque injuria*, which translated means 'harm without injury' or, as lawyers would say today, 'harm but not actionable harm'. Clearly the use of this Latin expression smacks of the argument by fiat to which I referred earlier in the lecture. It is important to note that we can develop a more systematic, theoretical argument against this claim for protection from or compensation for competitive losses, which runs as follows. There is a world of *social* difference between the harms inflicted by the use of force and those inflicted through competition. In the first case, we know that injury to the person and damage to property reduce the total store of resources available for human betterment. To make himself better off one party inflicts losses on a second person. That individual's reduced stock of wealth necessarily reduces the opportunities for trade that are available to third persons. The externalities from coercion turn from generally positive to sharply *negative*. However much a single actor might benefit from his own use of force, no one thinks that they can prosper in a society that generalises from that experience and allows all individuals to adopt the same practices at will.

In contrast, competition may cause harm to one rival producer but it also leaves his stock of labour and capital intact for a second transaction, and, by helping trading partners, it opens up new avenues to those individuals who receive goods at low prices and of high quality, and to the many third persons who stand to benefit in further transactions. To take a broad definition of actionable harm transforms liability from an occasional occurrence, such as a car accident, into an inevitable and ubiquitous occurrence. If A's success in competition is an actionable harm to B, then so too is B's success to A. A's claim only looks plausible when considered in isolation, but it looks grotesque when its full implications are considered.

Here is not the place to repeat the demonstrations that competitive markets maximise welfare by exhausting the gains from trade. It is quite enough to say that compensation for or protection from competitive losses destroys the gains from trade at every juncture. It may well be that the disappointed trader loses more from competition than from petty theft. But from a larger point of view, competition as a process produces systematic social gains while coercion and force as a process produce systematic social losses. The willingness to protect individuals against physical loss to person or property, or against defamation and other forms of molestation that involve either misrepresentation or threats of force, has the great virtue of allowing individual lawsuits to go forward when private and social welfare are perfectly aligned. But any offer of compensation or other protection to the disappointed trader has the exact opposite effect: it places a giant wedge between individual and social welfare. The point here does not depend on the particulars of the product or service that is offered. It is not undermined by the most painful stories that novelists can write about the havoc that demonic competition imposes on those who have found themselves displaced by market forces. It is a general proposition that is capable of general affirmation. It is one of those easy cases that it is absolutely vital to get correct: *there must be no compensation or protection against economic losses sustained through the operation of competitive markets.* It is a principle that is widely acknowledged and violated in practice.

3 COMPETITIONS AND CARTELS

The preconditions for competition are the same as the preconditions for cartels

In order to show the power of this general proposition, I will examine in greater detail two types of critical markets in which a strong political will could preserve the operation of competitive markets. These markets are agriculture and labour. In both these cases, the question of competitive harm has played an enormous role in shaping the legal rules that govern them. In both cases it is easy to envisage a competitive solution in which parties are able to buy and sell commodities and labour on whatever terms and conditions they see fit. In neither case do we have to worry about the need to create social infrastructure or to assemble complex networks through the wise use of government coercion. All that is needed is a willingness to allow prices to move in accordance with principles of supply and demand and to limit the use of monopoly power on either side of the market, which could be accomplished by a modest anti-trust or competition policy that focuses on horizontal arrangements to limit quantity or to raise price. To be sure, the anti-trust solution does not have an obvious libertarian pedigree, for it does not conform to the libertarian belief that the content of a contract is solely the business of the parties to it, and not the concern of any third person. In contrast, a classical liberal will share Adam Smith's distaste for monopoly and will distinguish sharply between it and competition. The classical liberal recognises the social dislocations produced by the former condition, when prices are raised above marginal costs and fewer goods and services are produced than in a competitive system. This bad result can be achieved when a single firm produces all the goods and services in a particular market, or when rival producers are able to organise themselves into a cartel, so that their production and pricing decisions replicate those of the single firm with monopoly power.

The social losses that flow from monopolies or cartels are capable of identification by economic theory, so that the central question is whether the tools that could be used to counter their effects are reliable enough to justify the costs of their imposition. In the traditional English system, these contracts to rig markets were not enforceable among the parties to them. The lack of state enforcement fostered a strong tendency to 'cheat' among cartel members, which tended to bring prices back to competitive levels. After all, each member of the cartel will do very well if it chisels a bit on price so long as all the other members keep to the higher price. But once any individual seller cuts his prices, then the others are sure to follow suit until the entire system falls under its own weight. The downward pressure is further exacerbated if new firms are allowed to enter the market under the price umbrella that the cartel creates. In essence, the minimalist strategy to deal with cartels is two-pronged. First, deny enforcement of any agreement among cartel members and, second, allow new entry, so that the entire system will sooner or later fall under its own weight. The more aggressive critique of this position is that this low-key approach will allow cartels to operate, and perhaps even to thrive, for limited periods of time. Their gains could be prolonged, moreover, if the rival firms merged because a unified operation would no longer have to worry about the cheating of any of its members. The more aggressive strategy, therefore, imposes sanctions on cartels, both civil and criminal, and allows the state to block mergers that operate, as the expression goes, in restraint of trade.

For these purposes, I do not wish to take sides on whether the more aggressive arm of competition policy has borne fruit. Much depends on whether the enforcement of these competition laws turns out to be misguided, so that it punishes firms that aggressively compete for business on the ground that they are engaged in some unlawful form of 'predation'. Much also depends on whether the evidentiary rules that are used to isolate cartels and cooperative agreements are sensibly enforced. If they allow too much collusive behaviour to slip through the net, then the system of anti-trust regulation is not worth its cost. If these rules catch by mistake too much pro-competitive behaviour, then the edifice turns out to be counter-productive. Resolving these questions raises a host of hard trade-offs that I shall, consistent with the theme of this lecture, avoid. But what is striking is how the development of agricultural and labour markets proceeds from quite different assumptions.

Here the law has done a total flip-flop on the question of legality. Far from condemning cartels, it has worked overtime to prop them up precisely because it sees competitive harm as something to be feared, not welcomed. Starting from that position, the law helps cartels by systematically countering the two risks to which any collusive arrangement is subject: the inability to police the conduct of its own members against cheating and the inability to block the entrance of new firms that bring matters back to the competitive equilibrium. We may have some uneasiness about the use of state power to enforce a competition policy directed against private collusive agreements. But whatever the doubts on that score, in principle we have no reason to reverse the policy in so dramatic a fashion in the two key areas of agriculture and labour policy. My greater expertise on these areas is chiefly with the US sources, but I shall refer to analogous British experiences to show that this dangerous tendency has truly international appeal, both historically and in the present day.

At this point, we have to ask why the forces within the agricultural and labour sectors were able to obtain that extraordinary dispensation from the state. Part of the explanation is technical. It is a sad but powerful truth that those markets that work best under perfect competition are also the ones that offer the greatest opportunities for cartelisation. Fungible products are helpful for creating competitive markets. Once products are standardised, it is far easier to have a large number of buyers and sellers in the market because the standardisation of products leads to an ease of comparison and substitution, which are the hallmarks of competitive markets. Thus, the ability to organise work in mass-production facilities creates opportunities for competitive labour markets as does the standardisation of agricultural produce.

Unfortunately, the flip side of the proposition is every bit as potent. The standardisation that allows for the emergence of competitive markets also paves the way for the formation of cartels, both by public and private means. So long as all sellers and workers are delivering the same product, it is easier for the cartel to coordinate prices and collateral terms. In contrast, in markets that feature highly individualised products, such as distinctive parcels of real estate, invariably there will be some jockeying over prices. Now the non-standard nature of the good creates a spread between the maximum amount the buyer will pay and the minimum amount the seller will expect. Accordingly, the parties will have to bargain out those differences. We need to live with friction in ordinary transactions even if we never learn to love it. Now when you have perfectly standardised goods, all of this tends to disappear because of the ability to find a perfect substitute by going next door in a business district that specialises in the same kind of commodity. The full information that makes competition possible in standardised goods is exactly the same condition that makes collusion work. If every seller knows that the rival sellers are selling exactly the same good that he is and for exactly the same price, the gains to organising this particular market to cut back production and raise prices (or wages) will make the privileged group better off, but the rest of the world worse off. First, they have to pay for this elaborate scheme to the extent that it is subsidised by tax revenues; and second, they now have to pay a monopolistic price or wage, which is higher than the competitive one. Additional complications will arise when price discrimination is available. But in our current reductionist frame of mind, it is best to put these issues to one side. The upshot is that we should see the greatest efforts at collusion in those markets that are most amenable to competitive solutions.

A moment's reflection, however, should show that these points are not sufficient to explain why the organisers of agricultural and labour markets were able to gain state support for their endeavours when ordinary manufacturers were subject to increased scrutiny of their behaviour. So much turns on the intellectual climate of opinion in which the legislative and judicial deliberations take place. Any political body contains many members who do not have a large stake on either side of the question. These people are neither agricultural producers nor agricultural consumers; they are neither employers nor workers, at least in the first instance. The ability to sway these neutral groups in argument often proves critical in gaining the necessary level of political support. The reason why people on all sides of the political spectrum are to this day so concerned with forums like these in which ideas are discussed and debated is because they know that their political influence will take them only so far. If public sentiment is strongly stacked against them, their options are limited. But if the political climate is congenial to their industry agenda, then their chances of political success correspondingly rise.

It is against this background that we can understand why appeals of farmers and workers could succeed while those of industrialists are turned aside, because, not in spite of, their greater wealth. Never underestimate the enhanced political sympathy when the underdog seeks to gain state power. Neither workers nor (individual) farmers are at the top of the income distribution, so they are perceived as having to struggle against greater powers on the other side of the market. In some cases, there may be a point here – for example, if railways are able to collude in order to raise the freight costs of shipping goods, some might argue in favour of creating a countervailing monopoly power for those that suffer.[1] However, in this situation the proper solution is to break up the initial collusion, not to create a rival monopoly that will be at loggerheads with the original one. But so long as people see

---

1   The buying power of supermarkets might be a corresponding example relevant to the UK.

the struggle between farmer and railways or capital and labour as a zero-sum game in which one side, by definition, wins and the other side loses, it is easy to make the underdogs favourites in the game of life.

But once it is realised that this simplified view of the world omits some key concerns, the persuasiveness of this maudlin plea should diminish. Successful cartelisation by any group not only hurts their immediate purchaser but also all the others who, in turn, purchase from them, including ordinary consumers who may be more down on their luck than the individual cartel members. In addition, the entire process is never a simple transfer of wealth from one side to the other, but part of an elaborate process that results in the systematic destruction of wealth from at least three sources: the creation of an inferior market structure; the political costs needed to put that structure in place; and the non-trivial administrative costs of making sure that the programme does not fall apart. At this point it does not make a difference whether the popular political forces are heard in Westminster, Brussels or Washington. They all sing the same tune about the simple distributive consequences of cartel formation which overlooks the long-term consequences of these arrangements. One cannot rectify the problems arising from an undesired distribution of income or bargaining power by creating more cartels, such as those in agricultural and labour markets.

4 AGRICULTURAL MARKETS, PROTECTIONISM AND CARTELS

A right to farm?

I think that this general analysis is borne out by a closer look at the agricultural and labour markets. Let me start with the American agricultural market in an effort to see how it sought to deal with the uncertainties that were introduced by fierce competition in a setting in which technical progress tended to increase output and, therefore, to reduce prices. Individual farmers knew that they could not alter that outcome by individual actions, for the laws of competition mete out harsh penalties to sellers who do not meet the competitive price. Raise prices and you lose your customer base; lower prices and you lose your profits. No wonder *everyone* wants public dispensation from competition. Indeed, in agriculture, if it is allowed to run without state intervention, rising productivity should lead to an exit of farmers from the market. This exit is welcome from a social perspective because it releases valuable resources for other more valued uses, but it is clearly not welcomed from the perspective of individual farmers.

Yet one of the great political successes of the agricultural movement is that it sought to insulate its members from the uncertainties of price fluctuations by appealing to the so-called parity principle, by which farmers sought to maintain prices at the constant high levels, relative to other goods, that they were able to fetch in the bumper years between 1910 and 1914. There is no question that fixed prices make life easier for farmers, but they make it far more difficult for everyone else who has to bear the full brunt of any fluctuation in supply and demand. Now the government has to use taxpayers' money to enter the market to soak up the excess demand, or it must find a way to reduce the level of production so as to maintain the prices at the desired level. Clearly strong subsidies and restrictions are needed to meet this unwarranted goal.

How is it, then, that any group is able to insulate itself from world uncertainties when that form of protection increases the uncertainty for everyone else? Part of the solution is rhetorical, with a strong appeal to positive rights. Thus, when Franklin Roosevelt introduced his second bill of rights on economic matters in his State of the Union address in 1944, this constant theme of 'the right to farm' was very prominent on his list and helped pave the way for post-World War II dominance by the farm lobby on agricultural policy. But what is meant by a right to farm? As an analytical matter, every assertion of a right should give rise to an instant query as to its correlative duty. Here the claim of a right to farm has to be set against two different kinds of correlative duties with vastly different implications. The first of the duties is that if somebody has the right to farm, nobody can block that person's entry or exit from the business. Hence, any farmers can offer produce for sale at whatever price to whoever they see fit, so long as they can find a willing buyer. So the right to farm reduces to a particular application the more general right to go into any lawful occupation: entry and pricing decisions are left to the individual alone. Deals, however, require a willing buyer. If that were all that was involved then the agricultural lobby would simply be working fiercely for free competition and open markets. Who could complain?

Of course, that proposition is not what they mean when farmers claim the right to farm. They mean that once they enter a particular occupation they have a right to remain in that occupation no matter what the conditions or what changes in demand or supply take place. At this point, the government's position or obligation is to make sure that any farmer can persevere as a farmer so long as he desires to remain in the trade. Major steps are made to insulate farmers from the powerful economic forces that engulf everyone else.

Agriculture as an 'easy case'

The system, however, requires not only rhetoric but specific economic measures to sustain it. Here, in effect, we find an inversion of the three central principles that organise economic markets: restraint of trade is now allowed; entry of new firms is blocked; and massive subsidies are used to prop up the overall arrangement. Easy questions, big errors. Here is a thumbnail sketch of how it all works.

One way in which to raise prices is to enter into contracts in restraint of trade. In principle, every single contract between two rival sellers could be treated as a restraint of trade, for it reduces the number of sellers from 1,000 to 999. But the key point here is not to deny that some small restraint in trade has happened, for indeed it has. It is important to stress the smallness of that effect, for given this change in market structure none of the remaining 999 firms obtains any real market power to set price or curtail output. Indeed, even this small change in market structure is likely to prove a non-event if a new firm takes up where an old one left off. Contracts in restraint of trade start to bite only when the level of collusion is high enough so that the few independent pricing decisions allow sellers to raise market prices. But the formation of a firm has a second effect that is much more powerful. It allows for division of labour and a specialisation of effort within the firm which makes this new operation a much more formidable competitor than the sole trader who has none of these advantages. The point here, moreover, neatly generalises because the system becomes better if everyone forms more efficient firms, at least until the concentration becomes so high that the balance of advantage shifts. The gains from specialisation are not likely to continue as firms become ever larger, but the risk of monopolisation grows. We have, therefore, to adopt some rule of reason that sets the 'horizontal' transaction against a backdrop of general economic theory from which we could conclude that a 100 strong and efficient firms will do better than a marketplace of 1,000 underdeveloped ones. The world is full of trade-offs, even on questions of merger.

Much of this learning has to crystallise around the phrase 'contract in restraint of trade', which will cover the giant trust but not the two-man firm. In the USA, the Sherman Act of 1890 marked the first federal effort to place a generalised prohibition on private efforts to monopolise various markets, and its reach was extended by the Clayton Act of 1914, which was passed under the 'progressive' influences in the early days of the Wilson administration. Here it is instructive to set out its terms for two reasons. First, it illustrates the close connection between labour and agricultural markets in the regulatory framework. Second, it shows the dangerous inversion of classical liberal principles, not because there is error on a hard question, but because it gets the easy questions wrong in principle. Here is the text of Section 6 of the Clayton Act:

> The labor of a human being is not a commodity or article of commerce. Nothing contained in the anti-trust laws shall be construed to forbid the existence and operation of labor, agricultural, or horticultural organizations, instituted for the purposes of mutual help, and not having capital stock or conducted for profit, or forbid or restrain individual members of such organizations from lawfully carrying out the legitimate objects thereof; nor shall such organizations, or the members thereof, be held or construed to be illegal combinations or conspiracies in restraint of trade, under the antitrust laws.[1]

This passage is rich in rhetorical power and symbolism. On the first point, the initial sentence refers only to 'the labor of a human being' – to which we shall return – because even the most ardent defender of cartels could not claim that agricultural produce did not count as a commodity or an article of commerce. But the consequences are the same none the less. Both labour and agricultural organisations are, in so many terms, exempted from the class of contracts in restraint of trade that run afoul of the anti-trust laws. The powerful differences among types of contract prove of critical importance, as this provision remains in force to this very day. Indeed, the same spirit that informs this section of the Clayton Act also influences the interpretation of the general Sherman Act prohibition against cartels and other contracts in restraint of trade. Where various groups who are not protected by the Clayton

---

1   Clayton Act, §6, 38 Stat. 730 (1914), 15 USC §17 (2000).

Act have worked to obtain the assistance of state governments in organising cartels for their produce sales, the question is whether this activity is caught by the Sherman Act. Here the answer at the height of the New Deal was 'no' in the important case of *Parker* v. *Brown*.[2] This case held that the decision of California to organise a raisin cartel for sales to citizens, mainly in other states, was immune from anti-trust scrutiny because the Sherman Act was in the first instance directed only towards private cartels.

The decision is remarkable for two reasons. First, the system in question misses the critical point that state-sponsored cartels are more dangerous than private ones precisely because the state enforcement reduces the (desirable) possibility of cheating by its members. Second, in this case the brunt of the high prices was borne by individuals and firms that lived or operated in other states. This was a case in which California was able to export misery elsewhere, just as the general blessing of export cartels in the USA under the Webb Pomerene Act[3] also places smaller amounts of domestic gain ahead of larger amounts of foreign dislocation. The political economy point could not be clearer: today the question of whether cartels are good or bad should be determined on a case-by-case basis. Yet no reason is offered as to why some cartels should flourish and others not. The strong classical liberal tradition may have doubts about breaking up voluntary cartels for fear its efforts could misfire, but this should offer no consolation to those who wish to prop them up with state power, as is done here. In any event, it is clear that American domestic policy sweeps aside in agricultural markets any principled objection to state-sponsored cartels.

---

2   317 US 341 (1943).

3   Pub. L. No. 65-126, 40 Stat. 516 (1918) (codified as amended at 15 USC §§ 61–6 (2000)).

The next question is whether this strategy will succeed. Here the basic answer is that an exemption from competition law, without more, would be most imperfect. There are two reasons for this. First, other firms could still enter the market under the umbrella that the cartel's price list broadcasts to the rest of the world. Given sufficient numbers, new entrants would bid down prices to the competitive level. Second, individual members could expand their output in ways that could escape detection, although this is less of a threat, obviously, when public funds are used to monitor the behaviour of cartel members. The next inversion of classical liberal principle, therefore, is that the incumbents must be able to choke off new entry and to make sure that the individual farmers still in business do not expand their production in ways that drive down the price. Here there are a number of techniques that help achieve this situation: acreage restrictions, for example, could limit the number of acres that individual farmers could place under cultivation. Or bumper crops could be purchased by government officials, again with a view to restricting the supply that reaches the market. Thus, the agricultural marketing order becomes the tool of choice to restrain supply.

Within the American context, however, this task was not easily done before and during the New Deal because of the constitutional impediments that arguably stood in the way of any administrative system of production restraints. The original design gave the US government only limited powers, the most expansive of which was the so-called commerce power, which provided that Congress has the power 'to regulate commerce with foreign nations, among the several states, and with the Indian tribes'.[4] The traditional view of

---

4   US Const. art. I, §8, cl. 3.

that power was that it allowed Congress to regulate the shipment of goods and people across state lines, but did not allow for the regulation of agriculture or manufacture, all of which took place within the individual states. The grant of the commerce power was intended chiefly to make sure that Congress could neutralise the barriers to commerce that individual states might wish to create in order to protect their own manufacturers and farmers from out-of-state competition. But the language of the clause was not perfectly congruent with that end, for the affirmative power to regulate commerce could be turned to restrictive ends, as frequently happened with the protective tariffs that were passed under the aegis of the foreign commerce power.

On this score one of the unanticipated developments in constitutional doctrine involved the judicial creation of the *dormant* or *negative* commerce clause, which stated that the case for a national common market was so strong that states could not frustrate its operations in the absence of clear authorisation from Congress. No state can stop your transport or your telephone wires from running across its boundary line. The upshot was that the Supreme Court took it upon itself to police the actions of the various states. Ironically, the doctrinal pedigree of the dormant commerce clause was far from secure, for an explicit grant of power to Congress does not automatically translate into an implicit limitation on the power of the states. But if we put those interpretative issues to one side, for the most part the US Supreme Court has done a decent, indeed near-admirable, job in keeping the lines of commerce clear while allowing the states, on clear and convincing evidence, to limit the importation of goods when they could establish a paramount local interest in health and safety, narrowly defined.

The point here is that because the court has shown a deep and consistent commitment to competition across state boundaries, it has worked hard to see that the necessary accommodations have been made, and has refused to defer to clever ruses that advance the cause of protectionism under such dubious banners as the ostensible indirect health and safety benefits from price stabilisation. Much of the engine of US economic growth can be traced to this one heroic judicial innovation, for Congress has on most occasions been slow to overturn state legislation that the Supreme Court has struck down. The federal system works when Congress is silent, and the synthesis that has been created under the dormant commerce clause is an appropriate model for the programme of the World Trade Organization or the EU today.

Changes in the attitude of Congress in the 1930s

The dormant commerce clause is not, however, the dominant part of the American story. Rather, the key developments of the modern welfare state involve the radical expansion of the affirmative commerce power. The basic decisions to cast aside the traditional limitations on congressional power came just after the court-packing crisis of 1937 when the Supreme Court switched course and held that Congress could regulate agriculture and manufacturing to the extent that they have, as they always do, an indirect economic effect upon the national economy. Once the floodgates were open, Congress responded in predictable fashion and the dislocations of the 1930s were largely attributable to two catastrophic mistakes. The first was the Smoot-Hawley tariff, an initiative to protect American business from foreign trade, which fell squarely within the scope of the foreign commerce power.

Regrettably, it was designed to allow for the creation of a tariff wall around the USA. The second was the steep deflation that increased the real debt of farmers and others by an unanticipated manipulation of the currency. In turn, it led to massive foreclosures and other dislocations, many of which preceded Franklin Roosevelt's rise to the presidency in 1933.

But little effort was made to attack these two causes of economic woe directly. Rather, in connection with agriculture, effort was focused on creating a nationwide cartel for agricultural produce, which did nothing to address the underlying structural difficulties but only exacerbated the whole situation by adding a third set of mistaken programmes to the witch's brew. That cartelisation effort could not be achieved by the individual states acting on their own, for the importation of produce across state lines effectively undermined local efforts to rig the market. Nor could cartelisation be accomplished by the national government under the restricted view of the commerce power, because in-state sales and home consumption of farm goods could undercut the restrictive effects of any national order. But at this point the US Supreme Court had lost its basic faith in markets, and thus could see no reason to restrict the power of Congress in an integrated national economy to attack these local sales and consumptions. As the marketing orders from the Department of Agriculture went out, the court in rapid succession first sustained the power of the federal government to regulate in-state sales of milk, which were undertaken in competition with milk marketed on an inter-state basis;[5] next, in what has to be regarded as a tour de force of constitutional interpretation, it held that Congress could regulate the feeding of grain

5   *United States* v. *Wrightwood Dairy*, 315 US 110 (1910).

to a person's cows under the commerce power even when there was no commercial transaction, state or inter-state, at all.[6] But in a weird sense its logic was unassailable: any leak in the restrictive wall would undercut the overall power of the cartel so the power of Congress to move had to follow the threats, even if these activities were as 'local' as one could imagine. And local consumption of grain could consume as much, I am told, as 20 or 25 per cent of local production. It is little exaggeration to say that the expansion of federal power in the USA, as far as agriculture is concerned, was to make the world safe for cartels.

The judicial resistance in the pre-New Deal era to state-sponsored cartels was manifest in yet another doctrine with clear English origins. To backtrack for a moment, the basic English position was that the owner of property could normally charge what the market would bear, where the clear implication was that competition by rival sellers would place an effective check on price. But at the same time the English courts, following the lead of Sir Matthew Hale, took the position that the state could regulate the prices in those industries that were 'affected with the public interest'. Those firms that had, either by virtue of government grant or natural advantage, a monopoly position were the prime targets of this prohibition. The position of Hale was relied on extensively in the 1810 English decision in *Allnut* v. *Inglis*,[7] where it was held that the operator of a Crown customs house, in which goods were stored for shipment overseas free of customs duties, could charge only a reasonable rate, for otherwise the increment in price could largely nullify the tax break that had been supplied by the Crown. That decision made

---

6   See *Wickard* v. *Filburn*, 317 US 111 (1942).

7   12 East 525, 104 Eng. Rep. 206 (KB 1810).

its way into American constitutional law in the post-Civil War period where it was used in far more complex settings to allow the state to limit the rate of return that could be charged by the natural monopolies in the network industries that emerged in the last third of the 19th century. Once again, there are many difficult questions on the permissible forms of state regulation: after all, if rates are set too high, then the monopoly can prosper, but if they are set too low, then the individual owners of the venture would not be able to recover a reasonable rate of return on their investments.

Subsidies, tariffs and protection

But as befits the temper of this lecture, I shall not stop to explain the ins-and-outs of the American doctrine. Instead, I shall turn again to the easy cases gone wrong. Somewhat oversimplified, the basic position of pre-New Deal American constitutionalism was that the states and national government had substantial power to combat the dangers of monopoly, but none to regulate the prices and rates that could be charged in competitive markets. The point here made good economic sense. Any effort to reduce the rates of competitive firms would in effect drive them into bankruptcy or confiscate their wealth. Any effort to increase their prices and rates would cartelise a competitive industry: the public loses either way if it is forced to spend resources on regulation in order to obtain an inferior outcome. But this sensible constitutional synthesis gave way in 1934 in *Nebbia* v. *New York*[8] when the Supreme Court on matters of rate regulation showed the same degree of agnosticism towards this doctrine that it was to show shortly thereafter towards

---

8   *Nebbia* v. *New York*, 291 US 502 (1934).

the commerce clause. It is no surprise that the transformation in doctrine was effected with an eye to allowing the state of New York to make it a crime to sell milk to consumers at less than nine cents per quart. A doctrine that had been designed to curb the power of monopolies and cartels was now reinvented to permit the state to strengthen their hand. It is again critical to realise just how much of American constitutional doctrine has been driven by the desire to make the world safe for cartels.

I have less to say about the third part of the inversion. As a matter of basic principle, the appropriate cases for subsidy are limited to those activities that generate some kind of public (or non-excludable) benefit for the community at large. Otherwise, subsidies in their own way distort competitive markets as much as restrictions on output. The individuals who bear only some portion of the cost of production will continue to produce goods until their private marginal cost equals their private return. That private decision will, however, yield systematic overproduction of goods because the additional public moneys spent do not generate social gains of equal value. The net effect is too many goods for too high a social price. The situation gets worse in the long run as the firms that do not make an orderly exit before the subsidy is supplied continue to press for its expansion long after it has been put in place. I wish that I could report that there were a series of American constitutional doctrines that sought to limit the ability of the states and national governments to supply subsidies to what should otherwise be competitive industries. However, the sad truth is that, as the constant wrangling in the World Trade Organization shows, it is a lot harder to define a subsidy than it is to define a restraint of trade, and harder to regulate subsidies even when they amount to direct subventions for the production of particular goods. For example, can we determine objectively whether providing good roads in agricultural areas is a subsidy to agricultural products? The constitutional history inside the USA is therefore much like the toleration of subsidies encountered elsewhere. Political forces turn out to be regnant and all too often they interact with tariffs and the domestic situation to produce a most ungodly situation.

I have no deep knowledge of the British or the EU tradition, but I have no doubt that the forces that have proved so powerful within the American context have manifested themselves on the other side of the Atlantic. There is, of course, no tradition of judicial review that might have placed brakes on legislative power. But the fundamentals are the same. The only way that the cartels can operate is by the restriction of entry, which means high tariff walls and powerful systems of national allocation. And any group that is powerful enough to organise protection can usually gain some direct or indirect subsidy. It takes only a peek at the current newspapers to realise that this free trade issue will not go away, whether it is manifested through debates over genetically modified foods in the EU or the US steel tariff, now mercifully lifted by a president but only after it has allowed economic wounds to fester for the better part of two years. It is a testament to the defects of our political institutions that positions that have so little to commend them intellectually are able to gain such political mileage.

Why, one might ask, do we see this regrettable set of results? I do not believe that it stems from any conceptual inability to perceive the dangers of protectionism in the abstract. The case against mercantilism and protection is one of the great achievements of Adam Smith's *Wealth of Nations*, which does not grow dim from repetition. But even if we put aside the emotional appeals made by discrete and identifiable groups that lose from competition, there is still another reason for the regrettable persistence of restraints in international trade: it is the problem of the second best. We can all agree that if all nations were to lift all trade barriers, all would benefit from the result. But what if the local faction of farmers in one nation or bloc captures the levers of power, and a similar phenomenon takes place elsewhere, perhaps dominated by the steel industry or owners of intellectual property? Here the issue of path dependence becomes paramount. Each side will demand liberalisation from the other before it is prepared to take the first step of its own. The interconnections between intellectual property and agriculture have been apparent in the international arena since the World Trade Organization's Doha round of talks, and the recent shipwreck in Cancun shows just how difficult these struggles are.

Unilateral reform would bring big gains

But even here there should be a clear course of action: declare unilateral surrender. The use of agricultural subsidies and trade barriers causes huge domestic dislocations right now. The USA, for example, would be far better off in its own economic well-being if it scrapped these programmes tomorrow, even if the rest of the world were determined to keep them in place. We could get the benefit of more goods and services in the USA, including those that are foolishly subsidised by foreign governments. We win, no matter what the rest of the world does. In this regard, it is useful to recall the great contribution of David Ricardo, who pointed out that the nation that imposes tariffs on imports hurts itself in the export market even if it invites no retaliation from abroad. The simple but ingenious point is that the relative value of the two currencies will not remain the same once the tariff is imposed. The shrinking demand for goods from abroad reduces the demand for the currency in which those goods are sold. The local currency thus becomes more expensive relative to the foreign currency, which acts as a price barrier to export. That cost is effectively avoided by a unilateral policy on free trade.

In looking at the wreckage of US, EU and world politics in agriculture, it is important to ask just how much this matters. In one sense, it matters less than meets the eye. The question of what goods are made available is a function not only of the political organisation that surrounds their sale, but also of the cost of production and the quality of the goods so produced. The raw products are only part of the overall price, and the incredible improvements in efficiency have driven down world prices so that the self-interested cartelist will find it in his interest to lower prices in order to maximise profits. The numbers here are huge: an egg costs about five per cent of what it did 100 years ago, because of ceaseless innovation at every stage of production, much of which takes place in ways that the agricultural cartel cannot identify, let alone reach. But before we rejoice in our good fortune, note that the gains from technology are not spread uniformly around the globe, and in some contexts do little to offset the advantages of climate and cheap labour found in less developed parts of the world. What has caused minor dislocations in advanced nations could wreak devastation in backward economies that can only expand if they gain access to developed markets. But then again this is one consistent cost of regulation. Democracy works on a territorial principle, such that those who do not vote do not really count, even if they suffer. What for us are small issues are for others matters of life and death.

5   CARTELS IN LABOUR MARKETS

Let us now turn to the labour market. To most people, any purported connection between labour and agricultural markets will be dismissed as fanciful. They don't seem to have very much in common. But initial appearances can mislead. First, the two are linked together in Section 6 of the Clayton Act, which at the very least suggests that there was an alliance between labour and agricultural movements. That connection is, moreover, not confined to surface issues. A look at the historical pattern of regulation shows that the movement in labour markets has followed the course of that in agricultural markets. It is important to trace out the parallels.

Freedom of contract in labour markets – another 'easy case'

Our initial question is: what is the ideal regime with respect to labour contracts? The first point is to note that possible weaknesses of a consistent libertarian position on taxation, infrastructure and collective goods and the like do not bear very strongly on labour markets. These are bilateral private arrangements that have little to do with the provision of collective goods. Twenty years ago I wrote an article entitled 'In Defense of the Contract at Will',[1]

---

1   See Richard A. Epstein, 'In Defense of the Contract at Will', 51 U. Chi. L. Rev. 947 (1984).

which offered an explanation as to why employers and employees might rationally choose to adopt a form of labour contract that allowed one side to quit and the other to fire at will – that is, for a good reason, a bad reason or no reason at all. The point is that if parties choose this arrangement the state should not second-guess that choice on the ground that it ought to supply workers with some greater measure of protection, which while beneficial to some workers once a dispute arises is disruptive to intelligent patterns of business behaviour. The acid test is whether an at-will agreement, or indeed any other kind of agreement, gives the best reflection of the joint wishes of the parties. In the overwhelming run of cases the answer is a resounding yes.

To make this point, my 1984 paper reviewed the standard attack on contract at will: the arrangement had to be inefficient because it allowed for arbitrary and capricious behaviour by management unrelated to the needs of the firm, owing to the inequality of bargaining power between the parties. The argument has an inexhaustible appeal, for it has been used to justify all sorts of regulation in labour markets, including regulations relating to minimum wages, maximum hours and employer discrimination. It has also been used to justify labour statutes such as the National Labor Relations Act in the USA. But the argument fails for one decisive reason. It is not plausible to think that just about every employee so misunderstands his interests that he enters into transactions that leave him worse off than before or do not reflect the value of his production to the firm. Here, as in so many other areas, free entry on the other side of the market affords the most powerful and consistent defence against arbitrary market power. Of course, there is little doubt that someone could point to some instances of the exercise of the power to fire that reflect the pettiness and incompetence of management, just as some decisions to quit are born of jealousy and ill temper. But the task here is not to examine under a microscope the aberrant behaviour of employers and employees in a few carefully selected individual cases. In a world of millions of transactions, it is always possible to fasten on the subset of foolish and resentful decisions, which will, it must be remembered, arise under any legal regime. Rather, the task is to find out what set of institutional arrangements will from the *ex ante* perspective produce in the long run the best set of results. Here the initial presumption that should hold in the absence of harmful subsidies or externalities is that common patterns of behaviour persist because they advance the interests of *all* parties to them. Customary practices between ordinary individuals will self-correct if they are inefficient, and the pervasive use of contracts at will at every salary level and in every occupation is strong evidence of the efficiency of the arrangement relative to its next best alternative. The one serious matter is to identify the source of those gains.

One obvious place is in the administrative costs, both public and private, of running this contractual system. These are low because neither side can force the other to continue with the relationship or pay some unspecified damages associated with the breach. In some instances, under a system of freedom of contract, either by custom and practice or by contract, an employer may supply severance pay upon dismissal, to give the worker some protection against dislocation. But this financial payment will be calculated by some simple formula. It will not allow courts to impose huge amounts of 'consequential damages' for emotional distress and economic dislocation. It involves none of the detailed exploration of the ups and downs of a relationship in the elusive effort to determine whether the dismissal was 'for cause'.

A second great advantage of the at-will system is that it supplies an informal method of bonding that keeps both sides in line. The employer who tries to take advantage of the employee by altering working conditions for the worse will be met by the threat to quit, for now the deal is worth less to the employee than the wage received. So long as markets are competitive the switching costs will be relatively low – lower in fact than they are in a highly regulated world where employers have to think twice before taking on a worker whom they may be unable to fire if things do not work out. Yet on the other side, the employee who takes it easy on the job is faced with dismissal because he is no longer worth his wages. But even here management will hesitate to dismiss for good reasons. One is the very substantial costs of recruiting and training a replacement who might or might not turn out to be better than the worker who was dismissed. The second is that unjust dismissals could induce other workers to leave while the going is good, thereby compounding the problem of recruitment and retention. (One sign of a well-managed firm is when departing workers are willing, even anxious, to help hire and train their replacements.) The pressures in any competitive market are always intense on both sides, such that the constant monitoring of each places a powerful check against the advantage taken by the other. Over time, as a relationship emerges, the two parties may well develop some level of trust in each other, which reduces the monitoring costs and allows them to make informal adjustments to preserve their relationship, adjustments that are far more difficult to make in any regulated environment. The at-will regime that is precarious as a matter of law often proves quite durable in practice. But where this contract falls short – as when one party has to perform first before the other must perform at all – then some new provision can be introduced to handle the defect. Thus, a salesman who is paid on commission cannot be fired with impunity after the account is landed but before the commission is paid. The at-will contract is a viable option, but it is not an obligation. Parties who want periodic or term contracts are free to enter into them.

A full regime of contract requires more than an intelligent law of employment contracts. The second critical piece of any common-law scheme of labour relationships must address forthrightly how competitors and unions must deal with workers under contract with other employees. The usual and correct rule is that any employee who works only under a contract at will is fair game for a rival employer who wishes to bid up his wages. The only way in which an employer can obtain insulation from this competition is to lock a particular worker in under a long-term contract. Thus, the effort to lure him away becomes a form of 'tampering', a tort or civil wrong that goes under the name of inducement of breach (as opposed to termination) of contract. At this point the employer with a long-term deal has a property right of sorts in the employment contract for its duration, which is protected only against those rival employers who seek to lure away an employee during term *with notice* of the contract arrangement. When that illegal inducement takes place, the current employer has, in addition to a breach of contract remedy against his wayward employee, the right to obtain an injunction and damages against the third party, even if he cannot obtain a decree that requires the worker to return to work. To give the famous English example from the 1850s, the worthy Lumley entered into an engagement with the famous opera singer Johanna Wagner for several engagements for the London season. The nefarious Gye comes along in order to bid her away. The court enjoined Wagner from working for Gye even though it could not compel her to sing for Lumley.[2] The point of the decision was to aver that competition is fine until people enter into specific engagements, but once they do they are protected from rivals. All in all, this system strikes a nice balance between the need for stability in labour relations and the need for competition in labour markets.

The development of cartels in labour markets

There are of course many refinements to the basic pattern which absorb the attention of the professional lawyer. But in line with our theme of the importance of getting the easy cases right, I shall pass those variations by. The central question for our purposes is how robust this common-law system is in the face of relentless efforts to cartelise labour markets. These efforts did not start with the large trade unions of the last half of the 19th century, but were much in evidence in the efforts of independent contractors (in contrast to employees) to organise guilds under state franchises and charters that would restrict output and raise rates for their members. Often these disputes translated into efforts by the organisation to stop the activities of individual members who wished to undercut standard rates. But the rise of mass-production industries demonstrated anew the proposition previously noted about agricultural markets, namely that those markets that are amenable to competition are equally amenable to cartelisation. Now that large numbers of workers are hired to perform similar jobs in the close proximity of the plant floor, the costs of organisation are relatively low when

---

2   *Lumley* v. *Gye*, 2 El. & Bl. 216, 118 Eng. Rep. 749 (KB 1854).

set against the anticipated gain. Here again the fundamental challenge for the labour movement is to find ways to organise its member workers while keeping out new firms seeking entry under the cartel umbrella.

Let's go through some of the steps in the process. First, there is the question of organisation itself. Can the labour union find ways to spur the coordinated activities of its members in order to raise wages above the competitive levels? Once this is done, the question then arises as to whether these kinds of activities should be regarded as contracts in restraint of trade, which expose union organisers and members to private suits for damages, public law enforcement or both. The late 19th and early 20th centuries saw a halting effort to apply the laws of conspiracy and combination against unions and their members. After all, what is the difference to third parties if the increase in the price of goods and services derives from employee as opposed to employer efforts to maintain cartels? By the mid-19th century it became tolerably clear in both England and the USA that the legislatures and courts were reluctant to carry this programme to its successful conclusion.[3] But there are some notable exceptions. In the famous Danbury Hatters case,[4] a union engaged in national secondary boycotts of the products of firms that refused to be unionised was held liable in a treble damage action under the Sherman Act, which resulted in personal judgments being levied against its individual members.[5]

The anti-trust laws were only one possible source of counter-pressure to unionisation. On the private side, of equal importance in this period in the USA was the so-called yellow dog contract

---

3   See, e.g., *Commonwealth* v. *Hunt*, 45 Mass. (4 Met.) 111 (1842).

4   *Loewe* v. *Lawlor*, 208 US 274 (1908).

5   *Lawlor* v. *Loewe*, 235 US 522 (1915).

(anyone who works for the employer outside the union was described as a coward or a yellow dog). This contract stipulated that an employee who agreed to work for the firm had to give that firm his undivided loyalty, so that he could not at the same time be a member of the union, either openly or in secret. These labour contracts were often on an at-will basis, so why, it may be asked, does the employer seek the additional stipulation from a worker who could be fired on the spot once his dual allegiances were discovered? The answer to this question lies in the issue of coordinated worker behaviour. Large groups of organised workers have the power to shut down a mine in an instant by a concerted walk-out of the sort that would count as an illegal collective refusal to deal under the anti-trust laws. But rather than pursue multiple and costly remedies against this group of workers, the yellow dog contract allowed the firm to bring a single action against any union for inducement of breach of contract before the collective action struck. Injunctive relief against the outsider was a powerful antidote to unionisation, but it left the workers the option, if conditions got too bad, to quit the firm and join the union. The English courts were prepared to extend the tort of inducement of breach of contract to the labour situation and the US courts followed suit. In its defence of standard common-law principles, the US Supreme Court, during this period, took two strong steps to preserve this common-law regime. First, at the constitutional level, it struck down, both at the federal and the state level, efforts to impose regimes of mandatory collective bargaining on firms as a limitation of freedom of contract.[6] Second, it held that the tort of inducement

---

6   See *Adair* v. *United States*, 208 US 161 (1908) (federal railways); *Coppage* v. *Kansas*, 236 US 1 (1915) (state laws).

of breach of contract applied to employees and unions in the same fashion that it did to opera singers and impresarios: an injunction could be obtained against a union so that it could not engage in covert organising activities.[7] The impressive generalisation makes perfectly good sense as a matter of general theory because in both these divergent settings the point of the legal system is to develop a set of institutions that favours and preserves competition both in capital and labour markets. Both these decisions, which have been commonly and fiercely denounced, should be understood as pro-competitive and not as anti-union.

Cartelisation and the political process in the UK

The political forces against this trend surfaced almost immediately, however, and manifested themselves in different ways in the UK and the USA. In the UK, the decisive movement was the passage of the Trade Disputes Act of 1906, which contained the following key provisions.[8] First, it insulated trade unions, as opposed to their members, against liability for tort. In so doing, it suspended the usual rule of vicarious liability that holds a firm liable for the wrongs of its employees so long as they arise out of and in the course of its employment. The effect of this provision was to immunise unions from liability even in the case of an authorised strike. Second, the act made the actions of individual persons undertaken pursuant to an agreement or combination actionable only to the extent that they would have been actionable without such agreement or combination. The point of this somewhat obscure position was to

---

7   Hitchman Coal & Coke Co., 245 US 229 (1917).
8   6 Edw. VII ch. 47.

state that the individuals could be responsible for acts of force and violence, which are wrongs when undertaken individually. But they could not be held responsible for any collective refusal to deal or secondary boycott, for in these cases there is no underlying act of force or fraud whose consequences are magnified by collective action. The net effect of this provision was, of course, to remove the anti-trust restraint on union conduct that fell short of the use of force. And finally, the act abolished in the context of labour disputes the tort of inducement of breach of contract and others relating to interference of trade more generally (as by force between potential trading partners). It also eliminated torts that interfered 'with the right of some other person to dispose of his capital or his labour as he wills'. The net effect of these provisions was to withdraw the legal infrastructure that was intended to secure long-term market competition. And just to finish matters off, the instability of markets was further increased by a generalised practice that denied legal enforcement to any labour contract. The long history of tortuous British labour relations was fostered by this legal regime, which had the continued backing of the Labour Party. The economic dislocations that this system inflicts are surely great, even if most difficult to calculate.

Cartelisation and its implications in the USA

In the USA, the traditional legal order held on a bit longer, given the Supreme Court's defence of the yellow dog contract. But alongside those judicial developments, the political forces of the 'progressive' era were pushing hard in the opposite direction to create labour exemptions from the complexity of contract and tort rules needed to secure competitive labour markets.

The first stage of the counter-attack was found in the Clayton Act of 1914, to which I referred earlier, which exempted all labour organisations from the scope of the anti-trust laws on the ground that labour should not be treated as a commodity or an article of commerce. This provision parallels the British Trade Disputes Act, and left labour free to organise for its own self-protection. There is, in this context, an instructive disconnect between the stated rationale contained in the Clayton Act and its particular legislative consequence. The normal consequence of stating that something is not a commodity or article of commerce is to treat it as a *res extra commercium*, or an item that is beyond commerce. That rule would apply to sacred objects such as grave sites and national monuments, and carries with it the consequence that they cannot be sold or mortgaged. But clearly no one in the labour movement wanted a rule that prohibited the sale of labour through ordinary employment contracts. What they wanted, and what they were able to get, was an exemption from the requirements of ordinary competition law. They also wanted, and were able to obtain, a general rule that prevented the use of injunctive relief in the course of a labour dispute, from Section 20 of the same statute. The effect of all this was to undermine the classical legal synthesis as it applied to labour relations.

Yet this system, for all its advantages, did not allow in and of itself for the effective cartelisation of labour markets because it offered no effective restraint on entry by other firms. Here there were a number of tactics used in manufacturing that were not available in agricultural contexts. One of these was picketing or patrolling, which is a devilish institution to regulate even under the best of circumstances. On the one hand, pickets could be regarded as individuals who supply information to the world about the practices of the employers whom they targeted and thus protected under any regime that prizes freedom of speech, including the First Amendment to the US constitution. But by the same token it is easy to see how speech can become hopelessly entwined with threats, or implied threats, to use force, which is unacceptable under a classical liberal order. Beefy workers standing en masse by a plant gate could use force against the entrants, and just that fear could keep people away from the gates. What makes the matter more difficult is that picketing could also be viewed as a collective effort to obtain a refusal to deal, which carries with it strong anti-trust-type implications, especially when used to organise primary and secondary boycotts. But even with all these difficulties, there is no question that picketing is one part of a comprehensive strategy to reduce entry by rivals that could otherwise prosper under the higher wage umbrella set by union negotiations.

In and of itself, picketing is probably not enough to switch the balance of advantage in labour disputes, for some people could easily treat it as a sign that the picketed firm offers lower prices than those that have the union blessing. In addition, picketing may fail to achieve its stated goals, even when it resorts to illegal activities, because it is expensive to maintain, and may not prove effective against rivals that may spring up at multiple sites. So here, as with the agricultural movement, it is possible to add new elements to the mix. For the most part this was not done in the British labour movement, but it was done in the American one. The first element was to withdraw the prospect of easy injunctive relief against labour unions, which was done in part by the Clayton Act and, much more systematically, under the Norris-LaGuardia Act of 1932, which also declared the yellow dog contract to be against public policy.[9] In addition, in 1935 the US system adopted the National Labor Relations Act. Importantly, this instituted a complicated administrative law system that allowed the majority of workers in an appropriate bargaining unit to designate a union as its exclusive bargaining agent, and established a set of statutory 'unfair labor practices' for employers who interfered with union affairs, discriminated against union members or refused to bargain with the union representatives.[10]

The effect of this system was to abandon the competitive labour market with rapid movements across firms. The intellectual set of mind behind both these statutes is easily observed in their statements of public policy. The Norris-LaGuardia Act treats as its public policy the assumption that the 'unorganized worker is commonly helpless to exercise actual liberty of contract and to protect his freedom of labor'.[11] The National Labor Relations Act for its part starts on the assumption of '[t]he inequality of bargaining power between employees who do not possess full freedom of association or actual liberty of contract'.[12] There is a certain irony in both these provisions because of their ostensible acceptance of the ideal of freedom of contract, which is said to be neither 'actual' nor 'full' for unorganised workers. The new implicit norm for a full and fair contract is the ability to exert monopoly power, and the correlative duty of the firm to bargain with workers who have opted by election for the collective bargaining solution. But the principle here is not capable of systematic generalisation. The employer in all cases has no ability to refuse to deal, but must

---

9   47 Stat. 70 (1932) (codified as amended at 29 USC §§101–15 (2000)).
10   49 Stat. 449 (1935) (codified as amended at 29 USC §§151–69 (2000)).
11   29 USC §102.
12   29 USC §151.

negotiate in good faith, without having to make any particular concessions to union demands. The system, therefore, creates a bilateral monopoly situation that is calculated to impose high transactions costs on unions and management alike. The law of good-faith bargaining has itself generated an immense amount of complex litigation as to the topics that must be addressed and the pattern of bargaining that must be followed. The firm, for example, that makes a take-it-or-leave-it offer runs the serious risk of being hit with a charge of 'unfair labor practices' under the act.

It is important to understand the major inversion of legal rules that is required by the adoption of this scheme. The most obvious change is in the law of contract, for now it is no longer possible for an employer to walk away from a transaction. There is a duty to deal that makes the standard industrial firm resemble a common carrier, with of course obvious differences, since there is no rate schedule typical of regulated industries. But once there is a duty to deal, the traditional rules of property have to give way as well. Employees have a right to engage in organising efforts that take advantage of the employer's property, at least to the extent that such efforts are not on the work-floor or during working hours. And the rules on speech become special as well. While the general American tradition calls for free and robust debate, labour law has its own tradition of speech in which the unilateral promise of benefits or threats amounts to unfair labour practices. These rules create immense difficulties in their application, but it would be a mistake to indicate that they have left employers utterly without resources on their own behalf, for the ceaseless debate over labour legislation before the National Labor Relations Board, and in the courts, has not allowed the union movement to run roughshod over a determined management opposition. But our concern here is not with the question of partisan advantage, but with that of social loss. While it is easy to imagine worse paths that US labour law could have taken, I am hard pressed to believe that this statute could produce any net social gain at all, let alone one that exceeds the extensive administrative costs of its own implementation. When one cuts through the endless details and complexities, what we see here is the statutory codification of a preference for monopoly over competition – an easy case wrongly decided.

To understand the full picture, however, it is necessary to understand the limitations as well as the influence of the National Labor Relations Act. This labour statute may create a state monopoly for the individual firm that has been organised, but it does not stop new firms from springing up in competition with them. The issue for the labour movement, therefore, has been how to block these new forms of entry. One strategy is to support various forms of legislation that make it difficult for people outside the union to underbid those in it. That decisive step does not, of course, protect the workers who are thrown out of jobs because they are not allowed to underbid their union rivals. The point here is to protect the union from competition by setting, for example, the statutory minimum wage above the competitive level that other workers could hope to earn, but below that which unions could through collective bargaining secure for their workers. Maximum-hour (and workers' compensation) law is a somewhat more complex story, for here these statutes, although apparently neutral, were prepared in a fashion that had a disparate impact on the smaller non-union firms, which had higher compliance costs than larger unionised establishments. In the UK, since Parliament was supreme, there was never a constitutional battle as to whether these statutes were consistent with either private property or freedom of contract. But in the USA it is no accident that maximum-hour and minimum-wage laws were subject to important constitutional limitations under the older legal order,[13] which also looked with hostility on any system of collective bargaining. But these constitutional limitations were quickly undone under the New Deal.[14]

Questions of individual rights were, however, not the only issues implicated in the US experience. The huge expansion of federal power under the commerce clause that I previously noted in connection with the agricultural cases was preceded by five years by an identical movement in labour cases. The earlier law did not allow for the national regulation of local manufacturing or agriculture,[15] and thus made it difficult for any state to impose a strong system of worker protection in the face of the exit threat. Earlier efforts to impose a national child labour statute had been rebuffed on the grounds that the federal government could not assume control over local matters by refusing to allow goods made by firms that had used child labour in their operations (not necessarily on the goods shipped) to be kept out of inter-state commerce.[16] Local governments did not refuse to enact child labour statutes, but sometimes allowed children to work at a lower age than any proposed national statute. But with the New Deal, the sharp change in attitude towards labour statutes carried over to matters of federal power. The lower courts all struck down the National Labor Relations Act as beyond the scope of Congress, but the Supreme Court broke with its earlier precedent and allowed

---

13   *Lochner* v. *New York*, 198 US 45 (1905).

14   *West Coast Hotel* v. *Parrish*, 300 US 379 (1937).

15   *United States* v. *E. C. Knight Co.*, 156 US 1 (1895).

16   *Hammer* v. *Dagenhart*, 247 US 251 (1917).

the statute to take hold.[17] The attitude that it was for the federal government to determine whether to support competition or monopoly became the dominant motif in both areas. In the end the labour movement was able to achieve its two major goals: the ability to organise its own members and the ability to get state assistance in the exclusion of rivals.

Restraints on union power

The question is then asked: what was gained by this powerful struggle? What is interesting from a comparative perspective is that the US system with all its legal requirements and administrative rigidities probably proved more successful than the British system that withdrew legal protection from labour relations altogether. Within the British system a determined union could exert enormous economic power without fear of disenfranchisement. Within the American system a number of powerful factors have tended to blunt the effectiveness of unions. First, the original 1935 New Deal statute was subject to extensive revisions under the Taft-Hartley Act of 1947. That statute was passed in response to the rash of strikes and industrial unrest that followed World War II and it tended to make the path of unionisation more difficult than it had previously been. A separate set of unfair labour practices directed towards unions was introduced into the statute, including a number that limited their power to engage in secondary boycotts. A widespread set of union corruption issues provoked further regulation under the Landrum-Griffin Act of 1959.[18] The judicial

---

17 *National Labor Relations Board* v. *Jones & Laughlin Steel Corp.*, 301 US 1 (1937), reversing *NLRB* v. *Jones & Laughlin Steel Corp.*, 83 F.2d 998 (5th Cir. 1936).

18 Labor-Management Reporting and Disclosure Act of 1959, Pub. L. No. 86-257,

interpretation of the statute has not been markedly pro-management or pro-union, so that the initial legislative compromises have by and large remained stable over the past 50 years.

In addition, the secular shift towards smaller firm units, which characterises modern economies, has complicated the task of organising workers. Most importantly, perhaps, the strong, if erratic, free trade impulse has exposed unionised firms to global competition even in such industries as steel, where the ill-considered tariffs imposed by George Bush in 2001 represented a most regrettable error before they were reversed at the end of 2003. The increased foreign competition in such industries as automobiles has effectively taken the strike option off the table for the major US producers because unions well understand that any strike for higher wages is likely to cause a major loss of market share or bankrupt the firm on whose success their own success depends. In general, I think that globalisation is the most powerful force at work here. If individual firms within an industry are not sitting on a secret cache of monopoly profits, there is little that a union can achieve, no matter how skilful its leadership or aggressive its bargaining strategy. The change in public sentiment towards free trade has had a very market-positive influence on the degree of labour power.

---

73 Stat. 519 (codified as amended at 29 USC §§410–531 (2000)).

6 CONCLUSION – THE IMPORTANCE OF GETTING THE EASY CASES RIGHT

In the end, everything is connected with everything else. Markets survive and societies prosper because they get enough of the easy cases right by embracing competitive solutions. It would be nice to report that these carry the day in situations where they should work well. But the experiences that we have had, and continue to have with labour and agriculture, indicate how difficult it is to secure a sound social result in the face of partisan and factional pressures that work to undermine it. In its place, we are all too often treated to the spectacle of complex legal arrangements that provide object lessons in economic pathology and opportunities for lawyers and expert witnesses to enrich themselves by working on disputes that ought never to arise in the first place.

Within the US and the European cultural framework it often proves very difficult to win the major intellectual battle over the dominance of competition, although I think it is a terrible mistake not to try. But it is possible to win some second-order decisions about the fine-tuning of these various systems which can mitigate some of their adverse effects. It is fair to say that, in terms of the agricultural situation, the technology improvements have partially offset political mistakes, at least in the developed countries. And I think that within the USA and the UK the new waves of technology and the expansion of the international trade system have mitigated some of the power of national monopolies. But this is not to say that we have reached, or are capable of reaching, a final resting place in the struggle between open competition and state-created monopoly. The settings that make competitive markets work well are the identical settings that make cartels possible. Our future success in picking the right policy option is, and will remain, dependent on the ability of people to persuade themselves that one set of outcomes is better than the other. Otherwise the political process will not support voluntary models but may in the end generate forces so strong as to gobble all of them up.

REFERENCES

Black, C. (2003), *Franklin Delano Roosevelt*, New York: Public Affairs.

De Soto, H. (1989), *The Other Path: The Invisible Revolution in the Third World*, New York: Harper & Row.

De Soto, H. (2000), *The Mystery of Capital: Why Capitalism Triumphs in the West and Fails Everywhere Else*, New York: Basic Books.

Epstein, R. A. (1984), 'In Defense of the Contract at Will', *University of Chicago Law Review* 51: 947.

Epstein, R. A. (1985), *Takings: Private Property and the Power of Eminent Domain*, Cambridge, MA: Harvard University Press.

Epstein, R. A. (1993), *Bargaining with the State*, Princeton, NJ: Princeton University Press.

Epstein, R. A. (2003), *Skepticism and Freedom: A Modern Case for Classical Liberalism*, Chicago, IL: University of Chicago Press.

Hayek, F. A. (1944), *The Road to Serfdom*, Chicago, IL: University of Chicago Press.

Olson, M. (1965), *The Logic of Collective Action*, Cambridge, MA: Harvard University Press.

COMMENTARY
Geoffrey E. Wood, Professor of Economics,
Cass Business School, London[1]

This essay by Richard Epstein, originating, as Geoffrey Owen notes in his foreword, in the 2003 Wincott Lecture, is in a field unfamiliar in Britain – that of 'Law and Economics'. In Britain these two disciplines are often regarded as separate. An excellent book treating law and economics as a linked and coherent subject (Veljanovski 1990) has been out of print for over ten years.[2] Few British universities offer even a single course on law and economics as a part of a degree, and where interest is shown it is often solely by lawyers. Economists by and large neglect the discipline, despite its importance in the work of, for example, the Office of Fair Trading. It is as well, therefore, to start by offering a definition of the field before proceeding to point out some highlights in Richard Epstein's fascinating paper and drawing from them some inferences of particular relevance to Britain, and to Europe generally, in the present day.

Cento Veljanovski defines Law and Economics as follows. 'The economics of law can be defined rather crudely as the application of economic theory, mostly price theory, and statistical methods

---

1   I am indebted to Charles Goodhart for his most thoughtful comments on an early version of this commentary.
2   I understand that the IEA plans to publish a new book on law and economics by the same author in the near future. This will be a welcome addition to the sparse European literature on the subject.

to examine the formation, structure, processes, and impact of the law and legal institutions.' He then goes on to separate the field into 'old' and 'new'. 'The old law and economics is concerned with laws that affect the operation of the economy and markets,' he writes, while the new '… takes as its subject-matter the entire legal and regulatory systems irrespective of whether the law controls economic relationships. In recent years contract, tort (the area of the common law which deals with unintentional harms such as accidents and nuisance), family law, criminal law and legal procedure have all been subject to economic analysis' (Veljanovski 1990: 14, 15).

These definitions are clear and helpful, but they are one-sided. They suggest that economic analysis can be used to help understand the workings and consequences of law. The subject is more wide-ranging than that. Law can help us understand economic outcomes and structures. In other words, we can either start as economists and analyse the workings of the law, or start with the law and show how it can affect economic outcomes.

The 'new' law and economics is the field of Richard Epstein's paper. What is the subject of the paper? Epstein's central point is that it is important to get certain big and straightforward issues right. The more complex issues, which attract much attention, while not unimportant – they can sometimes involve substantial expenditures – are unimportant by comparison with a few really big issues. The basic reason for this is that the 'hard cases' involve a great deal of effort, and still have a high failure rate. We can see with hindsight that the wrong decision was made, or, on other occasions, we remain unclear that the right decision was made. An example is the decision to build a new airport. Enormous costs are involved, and there are consequences for many aspects of life

– for 'noise, pollution, traffic, land values, business growth and the like', to quote Epstein. Such is the complexity of that one-off decision that it is easy to be wrong, even with the best will and ability in the world.

Before leaving these difficult one-off issues to one side, though, it is surely worth considering whether a way can be found of establishing a common framework in which to deal with such problems. By removing some of the 'one-offness', the costs of each decision would thereby be reduced. Surely a way of doing this which is worth exploring is to consider establishing, by law, a form of market framework; a sketch of such a one follows.

Those proposing to build a new airport (for example), and those opposed to it, could be required to register sealed bids, the first of how much they would pay in compensation for building the airport, the second of how much they would pay to stop it being built. Thus could be determined how much the airport was worth to each party if built on that spot; and whichever party offered more would make the payment to the other side and then have its way.[3]

What we do not have to live with, and most certainly should not live with, is neglect of easy cases that have important ramifications. What are these easy cases? The most important one, and the topic of Epstein's lecture, is: '… how a society draws the interface between market choice and government behaviour … The truly great social catastrophes … arise from a wholesale

---

3   This proposal exploits the Coase Theorem (1960) on externalities, avoiding the usual cost problem inherent in its use by restricting the scheme to where large sums are involved. It was the expense of such negotiations relative to the resulting benefits which led Coase to stress that his analysis revealed how to look at the problem of externalities rather than providing a universally applicable way of dealing with them.

disrespect for individual liberty ... and from a total contempt for private property...'. Be right on these big issues and much good will follow; be wrong and 'unnecessary social losses' are guaranteed and catastrophe possible.

He opens his argument on this by considering socialism and its associated collectivism as a means of organising production. Wholesale and complete collectivisation is and always will be a failure. If the required information were available to government it would become available to the citizens, who would try to undo the socialist attempt to separate what is produced from the distribution of that product. 'As the night follows the day, every clever government intervention will invite multiple private responses, which are certain to undo whatever good might have come about if dedicated government officials (itself a generous assumption) had exclusive use of the new technologies involved.'[4] It is unfortunate that Chancellors of the Exchequer and finance ministers more generally do not yet fully recognise this, for if they did they would abstain from the continual tinkering with taxes, incentives and regulations which preoccupies so many of them; but they do at least refrain from wholesale nationalisation.

Next he turns to the libertarian alternative. This starts from the presumption that '... voluntary transactions are presumptively preferred because they are positive-sum games from which both sides benefit'. For such transactions to be common and multiply there needs to be a framework of law to define and defend property

---

4   The observation about government officials may take British readers a little aback. The public choice analysis of government is both better accepted and more widely used in the USA than in the UK. Possible reasons for this are discussed in Capie and Wood (with F. Sensenbrenner) (2004); a major part of the explanation may lie in the traditionally non-partisan nature of the British Civil Service, at least until recently, even at the very highest level.

rights, for without such rights there can be few such exchanges of titles to ownership. The markets, Epstein urges, cannot generate these laws themselves.[5] He cites de Soto's example of street addresses, '… without which it is not possible to organise a system for delivering the mail or supplying electricity, gas, police and fire services'. That a framework of law is necessary is surely correct. We should, however, be careful not to concede government too great a role. De Soto's example illustrates the point well. London was the first city to have street numbers, following an Act of Parliament of 1765. But that act followed a private initiative. The first street to be numbered was Prescott Street in Whitechapel, numbered at the initiative of its residents, concerned to improve delivery of at least some of the services Epstein lists, in 1708.[6] Nevertheless, the scope for such private initiatives is limited to small groups – the costs of negotiating soon rise as the numbers of participants do, and inhibit non-government-organised action. We must therefore focus on how to judge and restrict laws.

Where, Epstein asks, does the 'simple logic of voluntary contracting' lead us in addressing this matter? His basic proposition is that there should be no compensation for losses incurred through the operation of competitive markets.[7] This was traditionally defended by lawyers distinguishing between harm and

---

5   Jonathan Sacks (2002) has also argued this position, with an only partially over-lapping set of analytical tools.

6   De Sotos's acceptance that street numbering requires state action is reminiscent of the acceptance of many writers of economics textbooks that the state had to organise the provision of lighthouses to guide ships, because these provided a good for the use of which charging was not possible. As was discussed by Ronald Coase (1988), in fact provision was organised privately, by groups of shipowners.

7   Asymmetries of information may in some cases produce qualification to this; but the existence of these is most plausible in financial markets, which Professor Epstein does not discuss.

actionable harm. An actionable harm, such as arson, destroys capital. Loss by, for example, not getting a contract as another supplier is cheaper does not destroy capital, leaves the firm that did not get the contract to transact again, and lets two parties gain from a mutually beneficial exchange. That is a brief summary of the economic argument Epstein advances for a legal conclusion. He then applies it to two important markets: that for agricultural goods and that for labour. Both these markets have been cartelised by government action, legislating with what no doubt appeared the best of motives but, Epstein demonstrates, to the harm of society in general.

Agriculture in the USA is supported by producer subsidies, as it was until recently in the EU. (The changes to the EU system which are soon to take place will break all links between current production and current subsidy; farmers will be paid for having been farmers in the past.) A producer subsidy system has to be buttressed by restrictions on production and on entry. This has served to keep prices unnecessarily high, and to inhibit the kind of entry that would promote consumer choice. Much of Richard Epstein's discussion of agriculture is based on evidence from the USA, but the EU's Common Agricultural Policy was at best similar (many would argue much worse) in its harmful effects domestically, and also did international harm. It did so politically, of course, by creating grounds for international disputes, but it also contributed to poverty in underdeveloped countries – for agricultural surpluses are shipped to these countries, thus destroying the fragile prosperity of their domestic farmers. Then, in further abuse of European taxpayers, taxes are spent in an attempt to relieve the poverty caused at least in part by the agricultural policy that residents of the EU are taxed to support.

Problems arise, too, in the cartelisation of labour markets which has been produced by legislation supporting trade unions and giving them immunity from many of the legal actions that cartels of producers would face. The result has been that unionised industries have maintained higher prices and innovated less in both products and production methods, and sometimes in consequence gone into decline that might well have been avoidable had their labour market been different. Examples admirable for the forcefulness of the demonstrations they provide are, first, Britain's formerly nationalised industries of gas, electricity and telecommunications, which have lowered prices and innovated when the joint labour cartels and producer monopolies were destroyed; and second, the British motor car industry, greatly reduced in size by competition from abroad, which had its life made easy for it by the rigid labour market of Britain's industry.

Of course, the biggest factor of all which follows from the 'simple logic of voluntary contracting' is free international trade. This not only maximises the benefits of exchange with any existing pattern of producers, but also moves these producers towards an efficient structure; for free trade injects into every economy blessed by it a virus – the virtuous virus of competition – which destroys monopolies and cartels through the entry of new firms. If a country has free trade then the harmful effects of protecting various groups through domestic policies are at least mitigated, and may well be eliminated altogether. Get free trade and much else good will follow.

Should we adopt free trade unilaterally, or should we, rather, adopt it only in exchange for similar moves by other countries? It has been traditional for economists to argue that unilateral adoption is desirable. Joan Robinson put the case with brevity and clarity; she observed that if other countries have rocks in their harbours there is nevertheless no reason to throw rocks into your own. And the same applies to tariff barriers as to such physical ones.

This conclusion is correct provided that there is no possibility that by negotiation the other countries will reduce their trade barriers. But as Richard Epstein points out, it is necessary to consider not only the impact effect of any measure but also subsequent effects. It thus becomes worthwhile asking what the impact of trade liberalisation made conditional on trade liberalisation by another country will be. An early example of this being taken into account is the repeal of Britain's Corn Laws in 1846. Sir Robert Peel, the then Prime Minister, was persuaded of the benefits of free trade by the economists of the time. (Frank Fetter (1980) provides an account of the parliamentary part at least of their activities.) The Corn Laws were repealed as an act of unilateral trade liberalisation. The action was unilateral because the countries of continental Europe would not negotiate to reduce their tariff barriers, and Peel eventually decided that it was in Britain's interests to liberalise alone. This led to Britain becoming a free-trading nation.

Peel hoped that Britain's actions would lead to what Bhagwati (2002) has called 'sequential reciprocity' – to other countries following Britain's lead, seeing how Britain had benefited from free trade and hoping to benefit likewise. There was subsequent trade liberalisation, but, as Richard Conybeare (2002) points out, although the liberalisation was clearly *subsequent* it is not possible to either confirm or deny that it was *consequent*.[8]

Are there advantages to actions that lead other countries

---

8   An extensive discussion of these issues can be found in Bhagwati (2002).

to liberalise their trade? Although a formal demonstration that there are such additional advantages is not straightforward, the intuition is clear. If two countries liberalise then each can specialise to a greater extent in producing those goods which it is comparatively better at, and consumers in *both* countries have cheaper access to goods that satisfy their tastes. Hence, although Epstein's principle that there should be no compensation for losses incurred as a result of the workings of a competitive market, and its natural extension that there should be no protection from the workings of such a market, seems to suggest that free trade should be adopted regardless of foreign behaviour, there is a case for multilateralism, provided that its end result is sure to be free trade.

This, it must be said, is not as easy as it may sound. Consider two countries entering into trade negotiations. One country wants both countries to achieve free trade, but will adopt free trade even if the other does not; the other is perfectly content if the first country achieves free trade, but does not wish to achieve this itself. If this second country knows that the first will eventually abandon protection regardless of the behaviour of the second, then the first has little if any bargaining power. Nevertheless, the game is worth playing. For free trade for both may be the outcome, not necessarily immediately or even after the first set of negotiations, but as the protectionist country comes to see the advantages free trade brings to both consumers and producers in the free-trading country. (Producers gain as a result of, among other factors, their becoming more efficient as a result of competition and thus doing well in markets outside their home one.)

The current trade negotiations at the World Trade Organization are an example where these issues should be thought about seriously by economists. We know that there are gains from unilateral free trade, and that there are even greater gains from multilateral free trade. These are among Epstein's 'easy cases'. What is harder is to determine is whether a multilateral or a unilateral course is the better one to pursue in any particular set of trade negotiations.

It is now convenient to move on to certain very recent actions of policy-makers, every one a consequence of neglecting Epstein's basic principles of supporting freedom of contract and considering subsequent as well as first-round actions, which although of apparently minor significance at present are likely to have numerous harmful consequences in the future. These relate to the limitation of working hours in place in most of the EU; the Trade Secretary's ruling in the case of the proposed takeover of Safeway, the British grocery chain; and recent changes to ticketing arrangements for London's buses. These are discussed in turn, before we return in conclusion to Professor Epstein's lecture.

Working hours were limited supposedly as a way of helping workers, and also, it was suggested by some, as a way of creating jobs for at least some of the large number of unemployed in parts of continental Europe.[9] This is of course another example of the interference with the labour market which Richard Epstein discusses. Interference with freedom of contract in this manner will impinge particularly on some types of workers and industries. Long hours worked over a period of the year, for example, are for some industries an efficient way of organising production. The workers in these industries (and in any industry where long hours

---

9   Explaining the fallacy behind the belief that by restricting working hours there will be a proportionate rise in the number of workers employed would be outside the theme of this paper. It is discussed in Wood (2002).

per week, although not necessarily every week, are an efficient way of working) are by this law made less productive. They will continue to be employed only if their wages fall. Thus they suffer rather than benefit from a law designed to protect them. The working time directive and associated labour market regulations are, in Epstein's terminology, 'easy cases'. They break the fundamental principle of freedom of contract – and in this case have the opposite effect from that intended.

The Safeway ruling moves us to some new issues, and also directs us to a section of Richard Epstein's arguments that we have not yet mentioned. It is useful first to outline the issue. A grocery store, Wm. Morrison, made a bid for Safeway. This triggered interest from other grocery stores. It was decided that a takeover could affect competition, so a review was undertaken by the Competition Commission. On the basis of this review, the Secretary of State decided that only Wm. Morrison could take over Safeway. This ruled out a competitive bidding process for the company, unless some bidder not in the grocery business decided to mount a takeover, and none did. Accordingly, it is highly likely that shareholders in Safeway will not do as well as they otherwise would from the takeover. Now, what are the objections to this outcome, setting aside the obvious one that shareholders in Safeway could make? What harm, except to them, has interfering in a voluntary contract done?

Suppose there had been no interference, and a higher price had been paid for the company. This would have increased the incentive in similar future cases for shareholders in a firm that was doing less well than others in the market to put pressure on the management to either improve or be sold. (Imposing such pressure is not costless, in either time or money.) This increased incentive would mean that the economy's productive resources were wasted for less time, and that is to the good of everyone, not just shareholders in the company.

To this argument that there should have been no intervention there may be opposed the claim that concentration in the grocery business would have increased as a result of such an unhampered takeover, and that such concentration would have reduced competition to an extent that could well have outweighed the benefits just described. It is somewhat contentious to claim that concentration reduces competition; it is the existence of barriers to entry which allows monopoly profits, and these barriers do not necessarily rise with the concentration of the industry. But be that as it may, an approach to cartels mentioned by Richard Epstein is relevant whatever one concludes on that issue. Do we need to worry about cartels, provided that agreements between cartel members are not enforceable at law, and especially if, in addition, new firms can enter the cartelised industry? There are arguments for this approach; and there are arguments that lead to the more aggressive anti-cartel policies of the USA and Britain. But as Epstein points out, whatever one concludes on this matter, the approach of considering legal intervention to prevent cartels is completely inconsistent with the attitude that has been taken to the agriculture and labour markets. The Safeway case involves a (relatively) minor issue, policy towards cartels. But it leads us to a big one. Allowing freedom of contract in competitive markets is of major importance; governments have recognised that principle. It is too important to be applied only where politically convenient.

Finally in these British examples, let us turn to one that is trivial by comparison, but which serves admirably to show the wide usefulness of Epstein's emphasis on supporting freedom of contract. It is now required of bus passengers within Central London that they buy their tickets in advance of travelling; drivers still check tickets and passes, but will no longer sell tickets. The advantage claimed for this is that it '… will speed up journey times for everyone …'. This is probably true. Where, then, is the problem? Essentially, the change requires bus passengers to have more information than before. They must have bought a ticket, possibly a season ticket, in advance, or buy a ticket from a machine before boarding. These machines do not give change, so advance knowledge of the fare, and exact payment, are required. This reduces the convenience of using the bus, so the efficiency gain claimed for shortened journey times should be offset by this cost. Why does the cost exist? Why is this change inconsistent with the principles Epstein lays down to guide contracting?

Because the change in contract terms has been imposed by a monopolist, consumers of bus services cannot choose between, for example, slower buses that require them to have less information and faster buses that require payment of fare in both cash and information. The difficulty has arisen because the market is not competitive, and because the contract is not entirely voluntary. This has both created the problem and made dealing with it hard. For how can we find out what to do? Would it be worthwhile, for example, to bear the cost of replacing machines that do not give change with ones that do?

The present system has no mechanism for finding out whether the cost of installing and using these machines exceeds the benefits they bring. As in the previous case, an apparently minor issue leads directly to a big one. By not having a competitive market we obscure information and have no way of finding an efficient solution. A 'hard case' has been created.

Professor Epstein's paper is a stimulating one, rich in powerful insights that can help us not only understand the world better but actually improve it and make every person in it better off, or capable of being so. Law and Economics is a discipline little studied in Britain, but it provides such a powerful set of tools that its neglect cannot be justified. I very much hope that this absorbing lecture encourages not only the use in Britain of the kinds of ideas set out in it but also the study and teaching of the subject, so that many of its practitioners become engaged in public policy formation and analysis in this country. This could not but improve both the laws that constrain private actions and public policy and the conduct of policy within the set of laws that constrain it.

REFERENCES

Bhagwati, J. (ed.) (2002), *Going Alone: The Case for Relaxed Reciprocity in Freeing Trade*, MIT Press.

Capie, F. H., and G. E. Wood with F. Sensenbrenner (2004; forthcoming), 'The Political Economy of Foreign Investment in the UK', in H. Huizinga and L. Jonung (eds), *The Internationalisation of Asset Ownership in Europe*, Cambridge: Cambridge University Press.

Coase, R. H. (1960), 'The Problem of Social Cost', *Journal of Law and Economics* 3(1): 1–44.

Coase, R. H. (1988), 'The Role of the Lighthouse in Economics', in *The Firm, the Market and the Law*, Chicago, IL: University of Chicago Press.

Coneybeare, J. (2002), 'Leadership by Example?: Britain and the Free Trade Movement of the Nineteenth Century', in Bhagwati (2002).

Fetter, F. W. (1980), *The Economists in Parliament 1780–1860*, Duke University Press.

Sacks, J. (2002), 'Markets, Governments and Virtues', in F. H. Capie and G. E. Wood (eds), *Policy Makers on Policy*, London: Routledge.

Veljanovski, C. G. (1990), *The Economics of Law: an Introductory Text*, Hobart Paper 114, London: Institute of Economic Affairs.

Wood, G. E. (2002), *Fifty Economic Fallacies Exposed*, Occasional
Paper 129, London: Insitute of Economic Affairs.

ABOUT THE IEA

The Institute is a research and educational charity (No. CC 235 351), limited by guarantee. Its mission is to improve understanding of the fundamental institutions of a free society with particular reference to the role of markets in solving economic and social problems.

The IEA achieves its mission by:

- a high-quality publishing programme
- conferences, seminars, lectures and other events
- outreach to school and college students
- brokering media introductions and appearances

The IEA, which was established in 1955 by the late Sir Antony Fisher, is an educational charity, not a political organisation. It is independent of any political party or group and does not carry on activities intended to affect support for any political party or candidate in any election or referendum, or at any other time. It is financed by sales of publications, conference fees and voluntary donations.

In addition to its main series of publications the IEA also publishes a quarterly journal, *Economic Affairs*, and has two specialist programmes – Environment and Technology, and Education.

The IEA is aided in its work by a distinguished international Academic Advisory Council and an eminent panel of Honorary Fellows. Together with other academics, they review prospective IEA publications, their comments being passed on anonymously to authors. All IEA papers are therefore subject to the same rigorous independent refereeing process as used by leading academic journals.

IEA publications enjoy widespread classroom use and course adoptions in schools and universities. They are also sold throughout the world and often translated/reprinted.

Since 1974 the IEA has helped to create a world-wide network of 100 similar institutions in over 70 countries. They are all independent but share the IEA's mission.

Views expressed in the IEA's publications are those of the authors, not those of the Institute (which has no corporate view), its Managing Trustees, Academic Advisory Council members or senior staff.

Members of the Institute's Academic Advisory Council, Honorary Fellows, Trustees and Staff are listed on the following page.

The Institute gratefully acknowledges financial support for its publications programme and other work from a generous benefaction by the late Alec and Beryl Warren.

The Institute of Economic Affairs
2 Lord North Street, Westminster, London SW1P 3LB
Tel: 020 7799 8900
Fax: 020 7799 2137
Email: iea@iea.org.uk
Internet: iea.org.uk

Director General	John Blundell

Editorial Director	Professor Philip Booth

Managing Trustees

Chairman: Professor D R Myddelton

Kevin Bell	Professor Patrick Minford
Robert Boyd	Professor Martin Ricketts
Carolyn Fairbairn	Lord Vinson, LVO
Michael Fisher	Sir Peter Walters
Malcolm McAlpine	Linda Whetstone

Academic Advisory Council

Chairman: Professor Martin Ricketts

Graham Bannock	Professor Stephen C Littlechild
Professor Norman Barry	Dr Eileen Marshall
Dr Roger Bate	Professor Antonio Martino
Professor Donald J Boudreaux	Julian Morris
Professor John Burton	Paul Ormerod
Professor Forrest Capie	Professor David Parker
Professor Steven N S Cheung	Dr Mark Pennington
Professor Tim Congdon	Professor Victoria Curzon Price
Professor N F R Crafts	Professor Colin Robinson
Professor David de Meza	Professor Charles K Rowley
Professor Kevin Dowd	Professor Pascal Salin
Professor Richard A Epstein	Dr Razeen Sally
Nigel Essex	Professor Pedro Schwartz
Professor David Greenaway	Professor J R Shackleton
Dr Ingrid A Gregg	Jane S Shaw
Walter E Grinder	Professor W Stanley Siebert
Professor Steve H Hanke	Dr Elaine Sternberg
Professor Keith Hartley	Professor James Tooley
Professor David Henderson	Professor Nicola Tynan
Professor Peter M Jackson	Professor Roland Vaubel
Dr Jerry Jordan	Professor Lawrence H White
Dr Lynne Kiesling	Professor Walter E Williams
Professor Daniel B Klein	Professor Geoffrey E Wood
Dr Anja Kluever	

Honorary Fellows

Professor Armen A Alchian	Professor Chiaki Nishiyama
Professor Michael Beenstock	Professor Sir Alan Peacock
Sir Samuel Brittan	Professor Ben Roberts
Professor James M Buchanan	Professor Anna J Schwartz
Professor Ronald H Coase	Professor Vernon L Smith
Dr R M Hartwell	Professor Gordon Tullock
Professor Terence W Hutchison	Professor Sir Alan Walters
Professor David Laidler	Professor Basil S Yamey
Professor Dennis S Lees	

THE WINCOTT MEMORIAL LECTURES

13 **The Pleasures and Pains of Modern Capitalism**
GEORGE J. STIGLER
1982 *Occasional Paper 64* £1.00

14 **Myth and Reality in Anti-Trust**
ARTHUR SHENFIELD
1983 *Occasional Paper 66* £1.00

15 **Economic Policy as a Constitutional Problem**
JAN TUMLIR
1984 *Occasional Paper 70* £1.00

16 **Two Cheers for Self-Interest**
Some Moral Prerequisites of a Market Economy
SAMUEL BRITTAN
1985 *Occasional Paper 73* £1.50

17 **Liberalisation for Faster Economic Growth**
Internal and External Measures Required
HERBERT GIERSCH
1986 *Occasional Paper 74* £1.50

18 **Mr Hammond's Cherry Tree**
The Morphology of Union Survival
BEN ROBERTS
1987 *Occasional Paper 76* £2.00

26 **Back from the Brink**
An Appeal to Fellow Europeans Over Monetary Union
PEDRO SCHWARTZ
1997 *Occasional Paper 101* £4.00

27 **The Conservative Government's Economic Record**
An End of Term Report
NICHOLAS CRAFTS
1998 *Occasional Paper 104* £4.00

28 **Understanding the Process of Economic Change**
DOUGLASS C. NORTH
1999 *Occasional Paper 106* £4.00

29 **Privatisation, Competition and Regulation**
STEPHEN C. LITTLECHILD
2000 *Occasional Paper 110* £5.00

30 **Anti-Liberalism 2000**
The Rise of New Millennium Collectivism
DAVID HENDERSON
2001 *Occasional Paper 115* £7.50

31 **Post-Communist Transition: Some Lessons**
LESZEK BALCEROWICZ
2002 *Occasional Paper 127* £7.50

32 'The Constitutional Position of the Central Bank'
CHARLES A. E. GOODHART
published with reissued papers by Milton Friedman as
Money, Inflation and the Constitutional Position of the Central Bank
2003 *Readings* 57 £10.00

Other papers recently published by the IEA include:

WHO, What and Why?

Transnational Government, Legitimacy and the World Health Organization
Roger Scruton
Occasional Paper 113; ISBN 0 255 36487 3
£8.00

The World Turned Rightside Up

A New Trading Agenda for the Age of Globalisation
John C. Hulsman
Occasional Paper 114; ISBN 0 255 36495 4
£8.00

The Representation of Business in English Literature

Introduced and edited by Arthur Pollard
Readings 53; ISBN 0 255 36491 1
£12.00

Anti-Liberalism 2000

The Rise of New Millennium Collectivism
David Henderson
Occasional Paper 115; ISBN 0 255 36497 0
£7.50

Capitalism, Morality and Markets
Brian Griffiths, Robert A. Sirico, Norman Barry & Frank Field
Readings 54; ISBN 0 255 36496 2
£7.50

A Conversation with Harris and Seldon
Ralph Harris & Arthur Seldon
Occasional Paper 116; ISBN 0 255 36498 9
£7.50

Malaria and the DDT Story
Richard Tren & Roger Bate
Occasional Paper 117; ISBN 0 255 36499 7
£10.00

A Plea to Economists Who Favour Liberty: Assist the Everyman
Daniel B. Klein
Occasional Paper 118; ISBN 0 255 36501 2
£10.00

Waging the War of Ideas
John Blundell
Occasional Paper 119; ISBN 0 255 36500 4
£10.00

The Changing Fortunes of Economic Liberalism

Yesterday, Today and Tomorrow
David Henderson
Occasional Paper 105 (new edition); ISBN 0 255 36520 9
£12.50

The Global Education Industry

Lessons from Private Education in Developing Countries
James Tooley
Hobart Paper 141 (new edition); ISBN 0 255 36503 9
£12.50

Saving Our Streams

The Role of the Anglers' Conservation Association in
Protecting English and Welsh Rivers
Roger Bate
Research Monograph 53; ISBN 0 255 36494 6
£10.00

Better Off Out?

The Benefits or Costs of EU Membership
Brian Hindley & Martin Howe
Occasional Paper 99 (new edition); ISBN 0 255 36502 0
£10.00

Buckingham at 25

Freeing the Universities from State Control
Edited by James Tooley
Readings 55; ISBN 0 255 36512 8
£15.00

Lectures on Regulatory and Competition Policy

Irwin M. Stelzer
Occasional Paper 120; ISBN 0 255 36511 X
£12.50

Misguided Virtue

False Notions of Corporate Social Responsibility
David Henderson
Hobart Paper 142; ISBN 0 255 36510 1
£12.50

HIV and Aids in Schools

The Political Economy of Pressure Groups and Miseducation
Barrie Craven, Pauline Dixon, Gordon Stewart & James Tooley
Occasional Paper 121; ISBN 0 255 36522 5
£10.00

The Road to Serfdom

The Reader's Digest *condensed version*
Friedrich A. Hayek
Occasional Paper 122; ISBN 0 255 36530 6
£7.50

Bastiat's *The Law*

Introduction by Norman Barry
Occasional Paper 123; ISBN 0 255 36509 8
£7.50

A Globalist Manifesto for Public Policy

Charles Calomiris
Occasional Paper 124; ISBN 0 255 36525 X
£7.50

Euthanasia for Death Duties

Putting Inheritance Tax Out of Its Misery
Barry Bracewell-Milnes
Research Monograph 54; ISBN 0 255 36513 6
£10.00

Liberating the Land

The Case for Private Land-use Planning
Mark Pennington
Hobart Paper 143; ISBN 0 255 36508 X
£10.00

IEA Yearbook of Government Performance 2002/2003

Edited by Peter Warburton
Yearbook 1; ISBN 0 255 36532 2
£15.00

Britain's Relative Economic Performance, 1870– 1999

Nicholas Crafts
Research Monograph 55; ISBN 0 255 36524 1
£10.00

Should We Have Faith in Central Banks?

Otmar Issing
Occasional Paper 125; ISBN 0 255 36528 4
£7.50

The Dilemma of Democracy

Arthur Seldon
Hobart Paper 136 (reissue); ISBN 0 255 36536 5
£10.00

Capital Controls: a 'Cure' Worse Than the Problem?

Forrest Capie
Research Monograph 56; ISBN 0 255 36506 3
£10.00

The Poverty of 'Development Economics'

Deepak Lal
Hobart Paper 144 (reissue); ISBN 0 255 36519 5
£15.00

Should Britain Join the Euro?

The Chancellor's Five Tests Examined
Patrick Minford
Occasional Paper 126; ISBN 0 255 36527 6
£7.50

Post-Communist Transition: Some Lessons

Leszek Balcerowicz
Occasional Paper 127; ISBN 0 255 36533 0
£7.50

A Tribute to Peter Bauer

John Blundell et al.

Occasional Paper 128; ISBN 0 255 36531 4

£10.00

Employment Tribunals

Their Growth and the Case for Radical Reform

J. R. Shackleton

Hobart Paper 145; ISBN 0 255 36515 2

£10.00

Fifty Economic Fallacies Exposed

Geoffrey E. Wood

Occasional Paper 129; ISBN 0 255 36518 7

£12.50

A Market in Airport Slots

Keith Boyfield (editor), David Starkie, Tom Bass & Barry Humphreys

Readings 56; ISBN 0 255 36505 5

£10.00

Money, Inflation and the Constitutional Position of the Central Bank

Milton Friedman & Charles A. E. Goodhart

Readings 57; ISBN 0 255 36538 1

£10.00

railway.com
Parallels between the early British railways and the ICT revolution
Robert C. B. Miller
Research Monograph 57; ISBN 0 255 36534 9
£12.50

The Regulation of Financial Markets
Edited by Philip Booth & David Currie
Readings 58; ISBN 0 255 36551 9
£12.50

Climate Alarmism Reconsidered
Robert L. Bradley Jr
Hobart Paper 146; ISBN 0 255 36541 1
£12.50

Government Failure: E. G. West on Education
Edited by James Tooley & James Stanfield
Occasional Paper 130; ISBN 0 255 36552 7
£12.50

Waging the War of Ideas
John Blundell
Second edition
Occasional Paper 131; ISBN 0 255 36547 0
£12.50

Corporate Governance: Accountability in the Marketplace
Elaine Sternberg
Second edition
Hobart Paper 147; ISBN 0 255 36542 X
£12.50

The Land Use Planning System
Evaluating Options for Reform
John Corkindale
Hobart Paper 148; ISBN 0 255 36550 0
£10.00

Economy and Virtue
Essays on the Theme of Markets and Morality
Edited by Dennis O'Keeffe
Readings 59; ISBN 0 255 36504 7
£12.50

To order copies of currently available IEA papers, or to enquire about availability, please contact:

Lavis Marketing
IEA orders
FREEPOST LON21280
Oxford OX3 7BR

Tel: 01865 767575
Fax: 01865 750079
Email: orders@lavismarketing.co.uk

The IEA also offers a subscription service to its publications. For a single annual payment, currently £40.00 in the UK, you will receive every title the IEA publishes across the course of a year, invitations to events, and discounts on our extensive back catalogue. For more information, please contact:

Subscriptions
The Institute of Economic Affairs
2 Lord North Street
London SW1P 3LB

Tel: 020 7799 8900
Fax: 020 7799 2137
Website: www.iea.org.uk